MW00667474

FUNDAMENTAL
IRON SKILLS

TEMPERING BODY AND LIMBS
WITH ANCIENT METHODS

戰鬥鐵
沙掌鐵
衫功協
會

FUNDAMENTAL
IRON SKILLS

TEMPERING BODY AND LIMBS
WITH ANCIENT METHODS

DR. DALE DUGAS

www.TambuliMedia.com
Spring House, PA USA

Disclaimer

The author and publisher of this book are NOT RESPONSIBLE in any manner whatsoever for any injury that may result from practicing the techniques and/or following the instructions given within. Since the physical activities described herein may be too strenuous in nature for some readers to engage in safely, it is essential that a physician be consulted prior to training.

First Published August 25, 2015
Copyright ©2014 Dale Dugas
ISBN-10: 1-943-155-119
ISBN-13: 978-1-943155-11-8
Library of Congress Control Number: 2015943528

All Rights Reserved. No part of this publication may be reproduced or utilized in any form or by any means, electronic or mechanical, including photocopying, recording, or by any information storage and retrieval system, without prior written permission from the Publisher or Author.

Edited by Arnaldo Ty Núñez
Cover & Interior by Summer Bonne

FOREWORD

Dale Dugas and I met 20 years ago in a Vietnamese restaurant in Boston's Chinatown. He was living in the area and studying traditional Chinese medicine and acupuncture and I was martial arts editor at Tuttle Publishing, recently relocated from their Tokyo office to their Boston office. We met for Pho and café sua da, and discussed kung-fu. We had a common friend between us, Renee Navarro, whom we talked about, too, and I found Dale to be full of energy and passion for the arts.

Jump forward to 2013 when I decided to start Tambuli Media. After the first book was published, *Mastering Eskrima Disarms*, I was in a martial arts supply shop and asked the owner what types of books would sell best. Immediately he said, "We need a comprehensive book on iron training." In an instant, my old friend Dale Dugas came to mind.

I reached out to Dale, who has been making quite a name for himself in the iron palm circles and making strides in selling his own brand of Dit Da Jáu, and asked him if he'd be interested in writing a book for Tambuli. He said yes, and in no time I had an outline in hand and we were on our way. A year later, with the editorial assistance of *Kung-Fu Tai Chi* magazine contributor, Arnaldo Ty Núñez, the book was completed and ready to meet its audience.

What I appreciate most about Dale is the common sense he brings to the subject of Iron Skills. The myth of iron palm training from kung-fu movies has finally met its match in his comprehensive book. No secrets! No mystical mumbo jumbo! Just a great manual for all serious practitioners of iron skills.

—Dr. Mark Wiley
Publisher, Tambuli Media
www.TambuliMedia.com

戰鬥鐵
沙掌鐵
衫功協
　　會

FOREWORD

After having spent four decades in the Chinese martial arts community, I have known both students and masters of various styles, systems, traditions and lineages. Considering this background, I have found Dale Dugas to be an exceptional individual. It is a pleasure to call him a friend and an honor to write this foreword for him.

Chinese martial arts are unique in their vast diversity. Technically, they encompass the four essentials skills of kicking, striking, wrestling and joint locking. In addition, authentic Chinese martial arts require an understanding of both the external and the internal. While today it is becoming disjointed; traditionally, Chinese martial arts were also linked to the vast Chinese healing arts tradition. To be a true master of Chinese martial arts requires decades of study and a wide breadth of knowledge. There are very few men that meet these requirements.

Dale is one of those men who have dedicated his life to Chinese martial arts. He has studied both the external and the internal; he understands their differences and their important commonalities. He is dedicated to the traditional but with an eye on progress and innovation. Perhaps most importantly, Dale's training in Chinese medicine and herbology makes him one of those rare men today who remain both a martial arts master and a master healer.

In the old days, a potential student would abandon their lives and travel miles to find a man like Dale Dugas. Those of us who were willing to do this are fewer and fewer these days. Luckily for the reader, in the modern age this is perhaps no longer necessary. In your hands, you have much of Dale's wisdom, without ever leaving your home.

—Sifu David A. Ross
NY Sanda and Lama Pai
www.SifuDavidRoss.com

戰鬥鐵沙掌鐵衫功協會

ACKNOWLEDGMENTS

I would first like to thank my parents, George and Nancy Dugas, for putting up with me when I was younger as I began my fervent training in the martial arts. It could not have been easy for them as I took to the arts likes a fish to water. I wore white pajamas while jumping around and yelling a lot. My poor parents; they thought it was a fad!

To my brothers, Jon Dugas and Dana Dugas, thank you for being my first training dummies.

Dr. Mark Wiley, owner of Tambuli Media, thank you for giving me a chance to share the knowledge that was shared with me!

Thank you must go to: Sensei Gary Young, my very first Uechi-ryu karate teacher, Sensei John Sullivan, and Sensei Jack Summers (RIP) who all taught me Uechi-ryu karate, judo/jujitsu, and boxing very well.

Thank you, Shifu Lee Yon for introducing me to Hung-gar kung-fu.

Thank you to Shifu Roger Hagood, who has helped me and many others to better understand Kwongsai South Mantis kung-fu. I am honored to know you and learn from you, sir.

Thank you to Shifu Richard Gamboa for being not only a close friend but also teaching me.

A special thank you to Ethan Brack, who posed for the application shots for me. Thank you, for eating the floor.

Thank you Dr. John Painter, Shifu Robert Castaldo, Shifu Andrew Garza and Shifu Alan Marshall, who all taught me much about Jiulong Baguazhang, Xingyiquan and Taijiquan.

A huge thank you goes to Gene Ching, Associate Publisher of *Kung Fu Tai Chi Magazine*, for publishing my first article on iron palm for MMA Training.

Shifu David Ross gets a huge thank you for giving up his precious time and allowing us access to his school for most of the photos illustrated in the book as well as writing the introduction. Thank you, sir! It is an honor to be your martial arts brother.

Shifu Arnaldo Ty Núñez, thank you for all the work on the book and advice on how to be a better writer. You are the best editor to have in my corner. Without you, this book would not have happened. Salute!

Thank you Sensei Russ Smith for opening your Burinkan Dojo for our first photo shoot. Although those photos did not make it into the book, I am grateful nonetheless.

I also need to thank all my teachers and training brothers/sisters in Japan, China and Taiwan, living and deceased, for all they taught me in Chinese medicine and martial arts.

The countless acupuncture, Chinese herbal medicine, martial arts teachers/practitioners I have met on my path have helped me become the acupuncturist and martial arts teacher I am today. I salute you all!

TABLE OF CONTENTS

戰鬥鐵
沙掌鐵
衫功協
會

INTRODUCTION

Most individuals in the West may not be familiar with the term "Iron Skills" or the Iron Palm. However, they have been exposed to facets of it via demonstrations of individuals breaking pine boards or slabs of granite at local martial arts tournaments or even on late night television and in film. Then there is a certain segment of the population that is familiar with the term, whose words would quickly resonate with various connotations depending upon the age group.

Some may recall the lovely Uma Thurman as "The Bride" in Quentin Tarantino's *Kill Bill Volume 2*, being instructed in the art of iron hand by the reclusive Pai Mei, which was played by the renowned Gordon Liu. But others would fondly recall the movie, which initiated the kung-fu craze in the West, *King Boxer*, and better known as, *The Five Fingers of Death*, which introduced the notion of "iron hand" to the masses. However, Mid-America's exposure to iron hand without being conscious of it was via the art of breaking in the late '70s with the appearance of an American Combat Karate master, Richard Barathy (1947-1996) on "The Tonight Show" starring Johnny Carson, "The Mike Douglas Show," and others. Barathy's most memorable appearance was the one on Carson's "Tonight Show," decked out in an American flag karate *gi* (uniform). He stood there, before 13 slabs of granite, which he lit on fire and in the process of breaking them he burned his arm; forever being enshrined in the annals of television lore.

However, the fans of kung-fu cinema are familiar with the notion of Iron Palm and Iron Body training and its devastating ability, which rings strongly throughout countless movies to the point that it has become the pinnacle turning point in the story. Usually, the plot of these movies consists of: A young man, who is the movie's hero, seeking revenge for the murder of a loved one; eventually he comes across an elderly monk or kung-fu master, who possess extraordinary fighting skills and lives in seclusion. The hero begs to be trained in the deadly arts of iron palm to average the death of his loved one. Through trial and tribulation the master concedes and instructs the hero in the secret art of iron palm, which later serves him in attaining his vengeance.

The training is typically depicted with the protagonist striking some sort of ridiculously huge training bag or worse, thrusting his hands into a wok filled with hot sand or even molten metal. The wok is naturally sensationalized by being superheated to a red color and underneath lies a roaring fire to give it that added touch of drama, which the hero grunts in pain, while penetrating the wok with his fingers. Then the student starts to condition his body by swinging heavy bags onto his chest or back and then striking a wooden post with his forearm or the shin of his leg.

Later on in the movie, as the hero engages in battle with the villain and at that climactic moment, when the hero is close to being defeated, he uses his hard-earned skill of iron palm to strike a particular part of the villain's body, causing massive hemorrhaging and instant death, which concludes the movie.

These vivid depictions of Iron Skills have caught the fancy of some individuals to the point that they have engaged in the training of Iron Palm or Iron Body without proper supervision; others have engaged in the art of breaking, again with no formal instruction, which can be physically and mentally harmful.

Real or "Wow Factor"?

One has to take into account that the art of Iron Palm, Iron Body, and breaking skills are a demanding process that takes proper training and sufficient time to make certain no crippling injuries occur to the practitioner. But, unfortunately, the media has taken this attribute as being the pinnacle skill that a martial artist can achieve. To the point; individuals like motivational speaker Tony Robbins, has used the skill of breaking as part of his life coaching seminar to empower others with the belief that breaking a board would assist them in breaking through their personal limitations and fears. An interesting fact is that Mr. Robbins is actually a Taekwondo black belt under world renowned Jhoon Rhee, who is considered the "Father of American Taekwondo."

At the same time, we need to be conscious that some individuals use the skill of breaking as a "wow factor" to gain fame or to embellish their prowess as martial artists. In spite of these extraordinary feats of strength, many of these individuals are not actually breaking for real. Some may wonder what this means.

The fact is, many who do breaking for demonstration to achieve the "wow factor" are actually striking objects that have been altered in some manner or other. For example, by using vinegar to degrade the cinder block's strength; baking the brick in an oven until it is brittle, so it can crumble easily with the slightest of touch; or simply using huge spacers between the striking medium. The spacers would facilitate an easier break because of the domino effect; breaking one slab or board creates a chain reaction that breaks the rest. It is much harder to break slabs of concrete or wood stacked one directly on top of the other.

In stark contrast to kung-fu movies and the media's portrayal, the art of Iron Hand consists of training with materials that are rather mundane compared to the superheated woks with raging fires beneath them. Real Iron Skill training was developed to preserve the body, strengthening and conditioning it to deal with the hardships of time. However, even though we are not technically preparing for the battlefield, the art of Iron Hand training still grants us benefits, especially for those individuals who are involved in pugilistic pursuits.

Beyond the Hand

Iron Palm training is actually one component of a larger canon, which is Iron Skills training—the subject of this book—which conditions the entire body for combat. This includes specifically, the hands, fingers, fist, forearms, torso, and legs.

Some may have seen Iron Body skills portrayed in the cult-classic film from 1978, "Five Deadly Venoms." One of the "venoms" was actor Gao Ji, portraying "The Scorpion" and possessing iron body skills—the ability to absorb impact to all parts of his body. In reality, such a skill is a crucial component of actual combat; be it in the ring or the streets. Simply put: you need to be able to absorb an opponent's impact in any encounter.

Essence of Iron Skills

In essence, the concept of Iron Skill and its training methodologies were designed to strengthen and preserve your anatomical weapons, which in this case are the hands, the torso, forearms, and shins. However, such training must be performed correctly, so as not to damage them to the point they become little more than useless nerve-damaged appendages.

The breaking of pine boards, cinder blocks, or even coconuts or a bat on one's shin is not the apex for training in Iron Skills; nor should this be considered anything but a simple pressure gauge within one's own Iron Skills training path.

The essence of Iron Skill training is a twofold:

1) To condition the body without getting hurt; be it for striking or absorbing a hit.

2) To develop penetrating ability when striking an opponent's soft body tissue or pressure points, especially at close-range.

The art of Iron Skills has been shrouded in secrecy—and worse, in ignorance—for so long that it has led to countless myths and apocryphal legends. However, in the chapters that follow we examine the methodologies that grant us the ability of Iron Skills without all the pseudoscience and ambiguity that foreshadow it for so long.

戰鬥鐵沙掌鐵衫功協會

CHAPTER 1:

BRIEF HISTORY OF IRON SKILLS

From the dawn of time, humanity has been forced to fight for their survival and in the process has developed various methods to train and condition the body to confront these adversities. One of the few civilizations that have survived since antiquity to the present has been the Chinese culture. It possesses a rich tradition in hand-to-hand fighting and the art of conditioning the body for combat. Several individuals have received, developed and passed along the ancient transmission of Iron Skills. We will discuss a few of them here, as they have direct influence on this author.

Gù, Rǔzhāng

Within the annals of Chinese's hand-to-hand combat stands out an individual, who can be considered the father of Iron Palm training in the Age of Modernism. His name is Gù, Rǔzhāng (1894-1952), and his notoriety came to be one autumn day in the newly inaugurated Capital City of Nánjīng, China, where he partook in the First National Guóshù Exam.

At the time China was still defining itself in the Age of Modernism (1890-1945). The political unrest that came from the end of Qing Dynasty (1644-1912) monarchy was still lingering. However, The Republic (1912-1949) was looking forward towards the future by balancing the old with the new, or in this case merging Western Culture with Eastern belief.

The youth quickly acclimated to Western culture; be it fashion, technology, sports, or calisthenics. However, individuals like Xú, Yībīng, Chén, Tiěshēng, Zhāng, Zhījiāng, and others were proponents of the idea that China's rich martial art heritage could be used to strengthen the body and spirit of China's youth.

These ideals gave birth to the Jīngwǔ Association (1910-present), which has been venerated within movies with its depiction in Bruce Lee's *Fist of Fury* (aka, *The Chinese Connection*), and three decades later by Jet Lee in two films, *Fist of Legend*, and *Fearless*."

Jīngwǔ in Shànghǎi, China, circa 1909.

Over two decades after the formation of the Jīngwǔ Association the Guóshù Institute was founded to spread the same ideology of strengthening the youth with martial arts. Shortly afterward they decided to organize a national exam with the objective to integrate the notions from past imperial military examinations, provincial lèitái challenges, and contemporary competitive spirit into one grand event to boost the warrior spirit of yesteryears.

Therefore, the First National Guóshù Exam was held in 1928, from October 15th through the 19th, in the newly inaugurated capital city of Nánjīng. An estimated 300 plus martial artist arrived in the capital city to participate in this one of a kind national exam. The first three days consisted of various demonstrations of hand-to-hand combat routines; displays of ancient weapon skills; oral examinations, which were akin to the imperial exams; and the finals consisted of lèitái matches (full-contact fighting on elevated platforms with no safety ropes). At the end, only 15 contestants survived these fierce matches and one of them was Gù, Rǔzhāng, who received the title of "guóshì" or national warrior.

Due to his achievements as a pugilist, Gù would go on to have a successful career as a professional martial art instructor through-out Southern China to the point he would be immortalized by two particular photographs illustrating his feat of Iron Palm. In them he is seen standing bare-chested in front of a stack 12 bricks and then breaking them with a slap of his palm.

By doing this, Gù became one of the first individuals who allowed himself to be documented displaying the Iron Palm skill, which was typically a kept secret of the shīfus. For those who are not

Legendary Iron Palm master Gù, Rǔzhāng, breaking 12 slabs

familiar with the term shīfu, it is a title of respect given to a master in various occupations. It consists of two Chinese ideograms: one, 師, which is pronounced shī and refers to the concept of a master. Second, the ideogram 父, which is pronounced fù, which means father or teacher. Therefore, this title is customarily used to refer to an individual with mastery in various occupations; be it a chef or in this case an instructor of martial arts. Indirectly, the phrase possesses the connotation of a surrogate father teaching a person a livelihood. For that reason, many of the older generation shīfu in China and abroad did not teach these skills easily nor openly and rarely ever taught it to non-Chinese. It was for family members.

This attitude radically changed in the late 1950s, when a certain shīfu at the time crossed the racial barriers and begun teaching his skills of hand-to-hand combat to non-Chinese and one of the skills that he taught was secretive Iron Skills.

Ark Yuey Wong:
Jim Anestasi & Ron Shewmaker

The first documented in-
dividual to break down
these bamboo walls was
a mild-mannered individ-
ual who ran an herb shop
in Los Angeles, CA. His
name is Ark Yuey Wong
(1900-1987).

Wong Shīfu came to prom-
inence for being a pioneer
in teaching Chinese martial

Ark Yuey Wong

arts and running a traditional Chinese medicine (TCM) clinic in the
early 1920s in the United States; first in the San Francisco Bay Area

and later in the City of Los Angeles. It
was in Los Angeles, where he would
teach the art of Shaolin Five Family
Fist, better known by its Cantonese
(Guangdongese) pronunciation, Siu
Làhm Ngh Gà Kyùhn, which he openly taught for over 50 years. However,
Wong would fondly be remembered
as the first documented shīfu to teach
publicly what is now commonly referred to as "kung-fu" to non-Chinese;
first by instructing Mr. Jim Anestasi in
1958 and shortly thereafter Mr. Ron

*Ark Yuey Wong striking a
heavy bag.*

Jim Anestasi, Ron Shewmaker, Ark Y. Wong, Chet, Paul J., Ralph Shun, circa 1962.

Shewmaker in 1959. They both would persuade Wong Shīfu to open his first public Móuh Gwún (Wáh Kiùh), which is Cantonese for martial (art) school. Prior to this Wong Shīfu taught privately out of his herb shop or in an adjoining parking lot.

One of the most unique attributes that Ark Wong would share with his students was the well-guarded secret and art of iron skills. He strongly believed that the art of iron skills was an integral

Ark Yuey Wong practicing the direct method of Iron Hand.

part in mastering Shaolin Five Family Fist, because of this sincerity and openness to teach others his art has become an enduring legacy that still continues to flourish throughout the United States, Mexico and abroad with numerous practitioners spreading his legacy in teaching others the art of iron skills and most of all Siu Làhm Ngh Gà Kyùhn.

Tim Yuen Wong:
James Yim Lee & Jim Novak

Beside Wong Shīfu, other Chinese would start teaching their respected arts to the Chinese community within the United States; one of those being Shīfu Wong, Tim Yuen, who would introduce a version Siu Làhm Faht Gà Kyùhn [1] or Shaolin Buddha Family Fist to the city of San Francisco.

In 1957, one of Shīfu Wong's students, James Yim Lee's (1920-1972), self-published the first English language book detailing the art of Iron Hand. The book was titled, *Modern Kung-Fu Karate: Iron Poison Hand Training, Book 1 (Break Brick in 100 Days)*. This individual's claim to fame, however, would not stem from this landmark publication, but rather from his association with the legendary martial artist and movie star Bruce Lee. However,

One of the first English-language books on the art of kung-fu.

James Yimm Lee demonstrating the art of breaking.

he should be remembered for his personal achievements in promoting Chinese martial arts and the skills of iron palm, which he introduced to Bruce Lee.

Lee's journey in Chinese martial arts started in the early '50s when he enrolled in The Kin Mon (Kihn Màhn) Móuh Gwún under the supervision of Shīfu Wong, Tim Yuen, where he would be introduced to the art of iron hand, which he would later document in his book titled. The book would remain as a testament of Lee Shīfu's instruction, which was progressive and safe, taught in a sequential way and included the use of liniments to protect the hand from incurring damage.

Emerging at the same time would be another remarkable individual; just like Jim Anestasi and Ron Shewmaker, he would also be documented as one of the earliest known non-Chinese to learn Chinese martial arts, and especially the skill of iron palm. He was Mr. Al Novak (1942-2011).

Al Novak demonstrating the art of breaking.

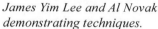
James Yim Lee and Al Novak demonstrating techniques.

Like James Yimm Lee, Novak began his training of Chinese martial arts at Kin Mon Móuh Gwún, which he later continued under the tutelage of James Yimm Lee, who in time would introduce him to the art of brick breaking. After a while, Al would assist in promoting James' book to the point where he appears in Karate Gi breaking a stack of bricks.

Eventually Al Novak would be recognized as an inspirational and knowledgeable shīfu who openly shared the knowledge that he had acquired throughout the years, including iron palm.

Without being conscious of the fact, these remarkable individuals would be the first to shed light on a secretive practice that has taken root on American soil from the time of the California Gold Rush (1848–1855). Their persistence and dedication has made these

The Shàolín Monastery.

secretive arts a viable tradition on foreign soils and for that we are grateful.

Myths and Legends

The skills of conditioning the body, especially the hands, have been an integral part of many Asian fighting arts. For example, Thai boxers are well known for conditioning their skins by kicking a banana tree, and Okinawan karateka are known for hitting a makiwara post with their bare hands. However, within the tradition of Chinese martial arts this training has been taken to another level by incorporating different methodologies to warm-up the body and to stimulate the blood

Bodhidharma

circulation prior to conditioning, and most of all the inclusion of various herbs to make certain that no injury occurs while training.

The tradition of Iron Skills can be traced back to the legendary Shàolín Monastery, which has been immortalized in print within the last hundred years and on the big and small screens since the 1980s. The Temple was originally commissioned by Emperor Xiaowen (467-499) of the Northern Wei Dynasty (386-535) in 477 AD for the Indian monk Bodhidharma (Bátuó, Damo) therefore, making it one of the holiest of places for numerous martial art disciplines, which trace their origins back to this legendary monastery.

Within those hallowed grounds many myths have emerged, but at the same time genuine traditions have also flourished there. One of those is the "72 Arts of Shàolín" which, like the monastery itself, has also been glamorized in print and celluloid.

English and Chinese copies of the "72 Arts of Shàolín."

The 72 Arts of Shàolín consist of an array of training methodologies to condition the body from the head down to the toes. Some methods are a bit exotic, like pulling nails out of a wooden board, and others are simple, like hitting one's body with one's own hand. Due to this, vast disparity in methodologies of training the body for combat has accidentally clouded practitioners' perception of what is real from what is simply fantasy. Sadly, this is due to the secrecy that has been inherent within the training of Chinese martial arts.

Withholding Secrets

Most of these methods were once considered highly secretive and only taught to long-term students or immediate family members. Over time, this led to the term "closed door" student; as many teachers would only teach advance material behind closed doors, believing that their art was too lethal and thus held in reserve for the chosen ones.

James Masayoshi Mitose hitting a makiwara.

Some teachers held back from completely transmitting their martial arts knowledge or in this case Iron Body skills for a wide variety of reasons. For instance, some teachers were afraid to teach these particular skills, because they were concerned that their students would inflict serious injury to an opponent or worse that the teachers would be held legally responsible for such behavior. This actually happened to the late James

Masayoshi Mitose (1916-1981), who introduced the art of Kenpo to the territory of Hawaii in the late 1930s. However, in 1974 Mitose was charged and convicted for a murder that he personally did not commit, which was actually committed by his student. In some accounts Mitose took the blame due to the tradition of an instructor being responsible for his student's action. [2]

Then you had some teachers that simply took their knowledge to the grave as they felt no one deserved it, and others taught a portion of their knowledge or worse watered it down, which is irresponsible, because it could lead to injury.

Secret Manuals

Certain systems of Chinese martial arts make reference to secret manuscripts, which contained the "seeds" or the theories of a particular style or clan. Usually, these books contained stylized poems, which are referred to as songs in Chinese. They typically transmit the elders' or teacher's knowledge about combat; be it is strategies or actual training regiments. However, some of these manuscripts were poorly written or used archaic symbolism causing further inability to use them as proper training

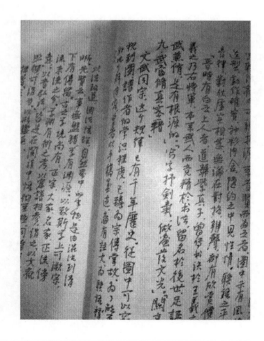

reference material, but within this information there were some gems, which possess real information.

By the early 1970s, some of these gems made it to the mainstream due to the kung-fu craze. However, many of these books were poorly translated into English. Some books were missing vital data; others depicted the training in a non-chronological order, or gave formulas for medicinal liniments or training herbs, which consisted of illegal or toxic ingredients that could be harmful if not used correctly.

---

1   Another version of the style already existed in Hawaii at the time, which was introduced in 1933 by Shīfu Lum, Dai Yong. Neither group is affiliated beyond possessing the same namesake.

2   The case has been shrouded with opposing opinions. In one account the judicial system did not understand the Asian ethics of a teacher taking responsibility for the actions of their student. On the opposing side, it was stated that James Mitose prompted his student Nimr Hassan to murder Mr. Namimatsu.

CHAPTER 2:

OVERVIEW OF IRON PALM TRAINING

Iron Skills training, when practiced safely and sanely, bestows a level of physical conditioning that is not found in the other pugilistic training methods. For instance, Iron Palm training will increase the bone and tissue density of the hands as well as condition all areas of the hand, which then can be utilized in any combative situation.

The palm is a versatile weapon, because it can be utilized in so many fashions. For example, the palm can be used to strike an opponent and at the same time it offers the ability to intercept or block an incoming strike. Then there is the back of the hand, which also can be used for striking and intercepting. As one can gather; the palm is indeed a versatile weapon and with proper Iron Palm training all of those mentioned attributes would be more powerful when facing others not trained in the art of Iron Palm.

It does not matter which area of the body one focuses their Iron Skills training, as this particular training would assist in increasing the density of the osseous and muscle tissue, which can help people as they age, besides its combative application. Strong and healthy bones are essential for hand-to-hand combat, but also for combating the effects of aging. Anything that can help preserve and strengthen your body is a good thing.

Another benefit in training in the art of Iron Skill is the development of a strong mind. A practitioner who trains these methods will develop a strong mental attitude. Therefore, learning and practicing these skills will create a steel trap mind that will be able to stay calm and focused throughout any situation, which is crucial to combat or any altercation in life, be it verbal or physical.

As one can gather by now, the art of Iron Skills transcends beyond its combat ability, but actually assists us as we age and helps us to remain centered in an ever changing and challenging world.

Parts of the Hand

To begin, let us examine the most commonly trained area on the human body, which is the hand, which we would refer to from now on as the palm. Therefore, the palm is divided classically into five areas:

1. **The center of the palm** is classically referred to as the *heart of the palm* or zhǎngxīn in Mandarin.

2. **The heel of the palm** is referred to as the *root of the palm* or zhǎnggēn.

3. **The back of the palm** is referred to as zhǎngbēi.

4. **The outside edge of the palm** is generally referred as zhǎngwàiyuán, but can be referred to as bèidāo.

5. **The Fingers** are referred to as zhǎngzhǐ

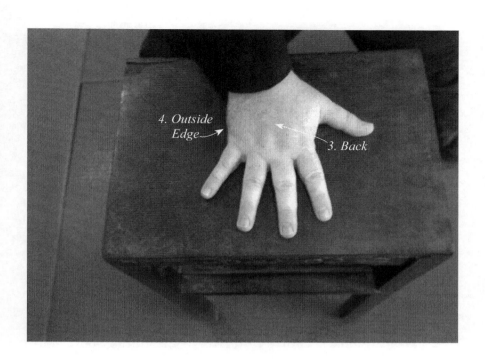

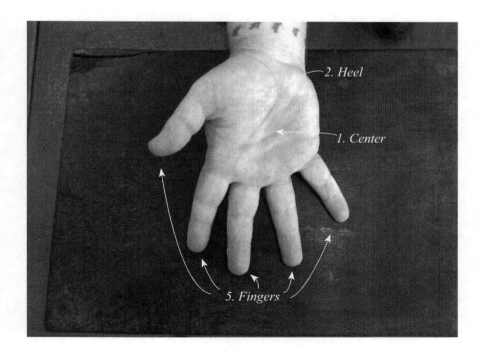

Why So Many Methods?

Some may say that variety is the spice of life. In the case of Iron Skills it's true, because one will see numerous methods and tools to achieve particular skills. Therefore, there is no one method, which is more authentic than another. As long the method in question does not harm the practitioner and produces the desired goals, it is valid. Indeed, each training method was developed to enhance a particular skill.

For example, there is a specific table, which has been designed to train a hand posture referred to as "tiger claw," which consist of the bending the distal interphalangeal joint and the proximal interphalangeal joint—in other words, making a claw shape with the hand. Therefore, the table is crafted to accommodate this particular training by being able to shift its top from a flat position to an inclined one. This makes it easier and more accurate to execute a claw onto an iron palm bag and being able to move it in an upward or downward motion, which are traits associated with the tiger in nature.

Because Iron Skills train various parts of the body and many different kung-fu styles have their own methods, one will see a wide cross-section of training tools used to achieve a distinct skill. For example, training can be done by striking one's own body; hitting a heavy bag; thrusting hands into buckets full of various mediums; and the list goes on. The most widely used implement is still a simple bag consisting of any number of different mediums, which can vary from mung beans (*vigna radiate*), gravel, pellets, sand, etc., with the objective being to condition the hand.

When hands are thrust into buckets of various medium, it is referred to as the *direct* method. When striking one's self or an object, it is referred to as the *non-direct* method. This book focuses on the non-direct method, which is recommended for beginners.

Usually the heart and root of the palm are favored in the beginning; especially because the objective is to develop penetrating power for an open hand strike, which is then followed by a strike with the back of the hand.

However, one needs to be conscious that some individuals have taken their training to levels which are considered improper due to the risk of damaging one's hand, which can lead to permanent nerve damage and a loss of range of motion (ROM) along with risking permanent physical structural damage of the appendages that have been over-trained or injured. Rather than harm yourself, use your training to strengthen and increase not only your skills but your physical well-being.

The Science Behind Proper Training

Before we actually begin to examine the actual methods of training, which some will consider as "forging of the body" into something stronger; we need to observe what is actually physically happening to our bodies. Iron skills safely and sanely practiced over time, will lead to a physical metamorphosis of the body parts being trained. However, unlike the aforementioned kung-fu movies, you will NOT develop an impenetrable iron skin or bones able to smash through people or metal structures without blinking an eye. Unlike those fantastical and unattainable fictions, what you will develop will be stronger strikes, blocks, and the ability to absorb much more physical abuse than someone untrained in these practices.

Western anatomists over the years have examined the stress factor that occurs in the body under the rigors of exercises and how it affects the bones and the tissues, which have been explained by two laws: Davis' Law and the Wolff's Law.

Davis' Law[3] is used in anatomical structures, and describes how soft tissue remodels after time under stress. It is the corollary to Wolff's Law[4], which applies to osseous tissue (bones). So when training the hands and other body parts as you do with martial arts and Iron Skills training you will inculcate a physical reaction to the stresses you are putting on the anatomical structures trained. Just like when you are holding a stance or using dynamic tension exercises, the muscle fibers stressed during Iron Skills training will actually thicken and remodel over time. The muscles and tendons of the hands, trained will change in appearance.

Literally the "forging" of bone and tissue over time will increase and give the practitioner more strength. As tendons are strengthened and thickened, bone and tissue density increase. This correlates to

_____

3   Pg 84 *Orthopedic Dictionary* Stanley Hoppenfeld, Michael S. Zeide Lippincott Williams & Wilkins, 1994 ISBN 0397513119, 9780397513116

4   Pg. 31 *Wolff's Law and Connective Tissue Regulation: Modern Interdisciplinary Comments on Wolff's Law of Connective Tissue Regulation and Rational Understanding of Common Clinical Problems* Walter de Gruyter, 1992 edited by Guenter Regling ISBN 3110875675, 9783110875676

having a harder and physically a stronger anatomical weapon at one's disposal, if needed in a self-defense situation.

There is no magic occurring, when training Iron Skills. No, an exponent will not develop skin or bones encased in adamantium. No voodoo-like mumbo jumbo energy strikes after meditating under the full moon for a year. In reality, you will have stronger bones as well as muscle tissue, which will give you the ability to absorb a much higher level of stress than a person who does not have this same level of physical conditioning.[5, 6]

You will be able to strike harder and block harder with your arms, legs and hands. This is why many Chinese martial arts systems continue to utilize these ancient strengthening and conditioning training methods to this day. One can see the advantage they would give you over those who are not strengthened in a similar fashion.

------

5   Chamay, A., & Tschantz, P. (1972). Mechanical influences in bone remodeling. Experimental research on Wolff's law. *Journal of biomechanics, 5*(2), 173-180.

6   Woo, S. L., Kuei, S. C., Amiel, D., Gomez, M. A., Hayes, W. C., White, F. C., & Akeson, W. H. (1981). The effect of prolonged physical training on the properties of long bone: a study of Wolff's Law. *The Journal of bone and joint surgery*. American volume, 63(5), 780-787.

戰鬥鐵
沙掌鐵
衫功協
會

CHAPTER 3:

INTERNAL TRAINING EXERCISES

Throughout the years Chinese culture has added new words to our lexicon, which typically have been associated with different foods. However, within the last 50 years new words have been introduced which are hard to translate into English without losing their true significance. In Chinese martial arts training, the terms Qìgōng, Wàigōng, and Neigong are essential to practice for holistic development; especially when training in Iron Skills. Let's look at them in more detail with exercises specific to Iron Skills development.

Qìgōng Methods

One term in particular is Qìgōng. Figuratively, it can be perceived as a breathing methodology, which can be coordinated with or without body movements. However, in Chinese tradition it signifies something more profound as it is the quintessential concept within Chinese cosmology.

The first logogram is qì, which can be translated as steam; like the steam emerging from a pot of rice. However, within Asian cultures *qì* is perceived as a cosmic energy, which can be deemed as bioelectrical energy within scientific terms. Thus, qì exist in all organic matter, which includes humans. The second logogram is *gōng*, which means achievement. When both logograms are placed together, you get the notion of working or training one's bioelectrical energy.

One should take into account this is a modest explanation of a very profound subject. Indeed, numerous books have been written on this particular subject. However, the objective is simply to give a basic introduction of Qìgōng due to its importance within the training of Iron Skills.

Therefore, Iron Palm Qìgōng consists of a series of breathing exercises—moving or non-moving postures. They are designed to stimulate the circulation of blood throughout the body, to reinforce joints, and to the center the mind. Typically, they are performed standing upright, while sustaining a particular posture with the arms. These are referred to as Zhànzhuāng or Standing Post exercises. However, certain postures can also be assumed while seated for those individuals that have difficulty standing for long periods of time. Below, two of the most basic methods of Qìgōng are introduced: "Everlasting Post" (Wújízhuāng) and "Propping-Up, Embracing Post" (Chēngbàozhuāng).

Everlasting Post

Everlasting Post helps to center the mind, regulate the breath, and develop and store qì. These attributes are associated to three areas in the body referred to as Dāntián (Field of Elixir). The lower Dāntián, which is known as Steam Sea (Qìhǎi), is located below the navel and develops and stores the qì. The middle dāntián, which is known as Man Center (Rénzhōng), is situated in the solar plexus and helps regulate the breath and stimulate the lower lumbar

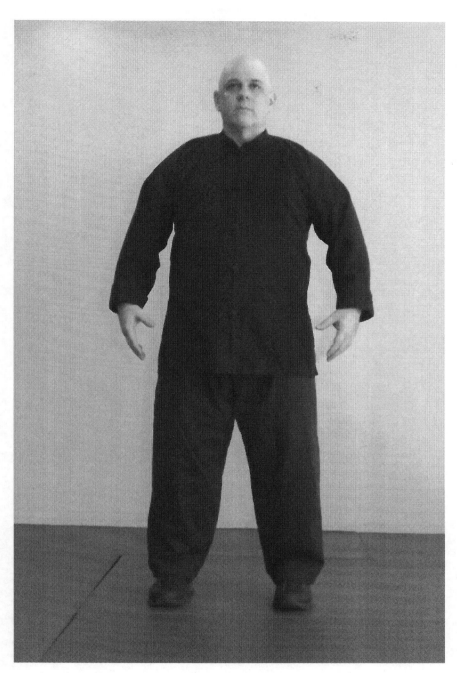

Everlasting Post

Propping-Up, Embracing Post

region. The upper Dāntián, which is known as Seal Hall (Yìntáng), is positioned between the eyebrows; here the qì assist in calming and focusing the mind. This method consists of standing with feet shoulders-width apart, which is referred to in kung-fu as the "two-character stance." In this position, the knees slightly flexed, and arms hanging naturally at the side of the legs.

Propping-Up, Embracing Post

The "Propping-Up, Embracing Post," which is also referred to as "Relaxing, Calm Post" exercise aids the body in relaxing like Everlasting Post, but at the same time energizes and reinforces the palms, the elbows, and shoulders with qì. Again, opening up a two-character stance; raise arms to chest level; mimicking a hug. Fingers are spread open and the heart of the palm facing inward towards one's chest.

Key Note: While sustaining these postures; the tip of one's tongue is placed upon the palate, while breathing through the nose; the mouth is closed. These particular postures will assist in regulating one's breath, which helps the body to relax and clear the mind.

Ideally, saliva will gather within the mouth, which means that you have connected two acupuncture points: Bǎihuì ("Hundred Convergences"), which is located on the top the head, and Huiyin ("Convergence of Yin"), which is located between the anus and the genitals. When these two points are connected, one is able to achieve an energetic connection called the microcosmic orbit, and inner calmness.

These qìgōng exercise postures should be done prior to training the other qìgōng exercises. Ideally, each posture should be sustained for two-minutes. In the beginning, however, it is recommended to sustain the postures for just one minute to acclimate the body and the mind being still; this is not an easy task. This assists the body to remove residual tension, which in turn makes us healthier by lowering blood pressure and actually improving our reflects. A great advantage of these exercises; that they can be utilized beyond the practice of Iron Palm and used to improve one's health.

Wàigōng Methods

The first two sets of qìgōng exercises that you were introduced to are referred to as a Nèigōng or "Internal Achievement." The objective of these particular exercises is to coordinate one's breathing with subtle body movements without straining or tensing the muscles. As there is a soft, there is a hard; therefore, you have wàigōng or external achievement, which typically utilizes some of form of isometric notion (i.e., contracting the muscles in coordination with one's breath). Therefore, after completing the Standing Post exercises you then move on to the wàigōng exercises referred to as: Bàoquán or "Embracing Fist" and Hēilóngbǎiwěi or "Black Dragon Swinging Tail." Let's look at them below.

Embracing Fist (Bàoquán)

The objective of Embracing Fist is to contract the arm muscles while clenching the fists. This assists in concentrating blood in the area of the hand and arm, which in turn warms up the muscles. First, you will open your legs to form a horse stance or mǎbù. To

Horse Stance

Horse Stance, Embracing Fist

Horse Stance, Post Arm

Horse Stance, Lifting Fist

Horse Stance, Sinking Arm

Horse Stance, Pushing Palm

Horse Stance, Seizing Hand

Horse Stance, Embracing Fist 1

Horse Stance, Embracing Fist 2

Horse Stance, Post Fist

Horse Stance, Lifting Fist

Horse Stance, Sinking Arm

Horse Stance, Pushing Palm

Horse Stance, Seizing Hand

Horse Stance, Embracing Fist 1

Horse Stance, Embracing Fist 2

assume this stance, simply separate the feet such that they are parallel to one another with the knees slightly bent. The knees should be on vertical plain, perpendicular with the toes, but not exceeding over them. Clenched hands are held at the hips, keeping the body up right and the eyes level.

Ideally, the width of your stance should be 2.5 times the width of your shoulders. Now slowly squat down to about 20% into your stance, until you can feel a slight pressure in your quadriceps (thigh) muscles. Then curl one of your arms up to your elbow while the upper arm are in alignment with your shoulders, which is referred to as Post Arm.

You then pull the arm back so that now your upper arm is aligned with your shoulder at a 90° angle from where you are facing. Then pull the elbow down to your side, and when you touch the side of your body with your elbow you will open your hand into an open palm.

Then push with your palm, which is on the side of your body, outwardly to the front of your body until the palms are facing in front of you. When you get the arm extended out to the front, you will then take your fingers and one at a time curl them into fists. Then you rotate the fists so that the palm faces the ceiling, and pull your arms back to the hips from where you started. This would be considered one repetition. Now repeat the sequence on the opposite arm; in this case the left one.

Ideally, you should start with 10 repetitions on each hand, which means you will start with a total of 20 reps the first week of your training. You will want to add 10 reps each week until you get to a total of 50 reps per arm. I was actually taught there was no need to go beyond 50 reps (100 actual repetitions split between the left and right arms) to achieve the desired ability.

These particular arm movements are coordinated with a particular breathing pattern, which is done as such:

- ❖ Inhale while curling the arm up and out toward the side of your body, completing the inhalation as the arm comes down to the side of the body.

- ❖ Exhale as you open the palm and start to push the arm out towards the front.

Key Note: Do not rush your breathing or the movement. Use minimum amount of tension. Too much tension will cause you to overexert and get very tight in the arms and upper chest and back quickly, which is counterproductive to the desired results. The objective is to warm up the arms; not work them as hard as you can. This exercise is great to do beyond warming up for Iron Palm training; for example, by adding more tension one is able to increase one's arm strength. However, never use too much tension that your arm starts to shake and make certain that your breathing is in sync with the movements.

Black Dragon Swings Tail

The second Wàigōng routine is designed to release tension from the arms and the hands and is done after striking the bags; it is referred to as Black Dragon Swings Tail.

Black Dragon Swings Tail 1

Black Dragon Swings Tail 2

Black Dragon Swings Tail 3

Black Dragon Swings Tail 4

First, open up to a Two-Character Stance, then lift the arms, while bringing up your elbows; so that they are pointing out away from the body. Your hands will be in, towards the chest with the fingers touching the sternum. Next, pull the elbows away from the body, while unfolding the arms and the hand flicks out to the sides.

Key Note: Do not use added tension or over accelerate the motion; be cautious to lead with the elbows and not the hand, because the motion is generated by the elbow and not the hands. Leading with the hands can accidentally result in hyper-extension of the elbows. Therefore, lead the motion with the elbows, pressing them out towards the sides of the body, unfolding the arms and then flicking the hands out to the sides; as if flicking water off the fingers. At this moment you want to exhale from the belly— squeezing the belly like it was a bellows, slightly, hissing (i.e., Sii), through your closed teeth, while exhaling. This will help release tension from the tendons of the arms, as well as imparting the ability to strike with the back of your hands, which is referred to as a Floating Palm.

Nèigōng Methods

After completing the above two wàigōng exercises, you move forward to three Nèigōng exercises, which are referred to as Sānfǎhéngqì or "Three Methods Balancing Steam" (energy).

These exercises are designed to help ingrain particular movements within the body as well as facilitate a deeper sense of relaxation and a calmer state of being, especially after completing the wàigōng, which put some strain on the body. Therefore, these exercises are meant to relax the body and at the same time develop a notion referred to in the classics as *yì* or intent. The objective is to focus on the movement you are executing; how it is being formed and its functions. Therefore, in the beginning the objective is to move the qì from its centralized location at the center mass of the body, which is referred to as the dāntián, up the spine, and bringing it up to the top of the head, and then dividing the energy to circulate down both arms and finally down to the palms.

Key Note: Do not try to push the energy, which should be felt as a warm or tingling sensation in the arms. Do not force anything. Just feel it move into the hands; this is considered the "pathway," which encourages the opening of the body.

This particular training method in training your awareness level as well as your ability to focus. You will develop a steel trap mind. There is a training maxim that states: "The Mind Commands, The Body Responds, and The Energy Follows." Therefore, train the mind/intent and everything else will fall into place.

The Three Methods Balancing Steam is divided into the following three exercises: 1) Pressing Heaven, 2) Pressing Earth, and 3) Pressing Heaven and Earth. These exercises should be executed within a Two-Character Stance, which is also referred to as wújíbù or non-extremities stance. Make certain to tuck the hips slightly under the torso as if you are trying to sit on a stool.

You will be employing this stance for all the following three nèigōng exercises; which do not utilize your lower body (i.e., there should be no moving or shifting). All movement will be generated from your upper body/arms, which should be coordinated with your breath from beginning to end of the movement. The objective is to move slowly and to exhale at the conclusion of the arm motion; do not accelerate or hyperventilate.

Pressing Heaven

The first exercise in this group is called "Pressing Heaven." First, take your hands and place them with your fingers pointing at each other in front of your forehead with your palms facing away from you; now inhale. Then slowly start to extend the arms above the head; do not move anything other than your arms.

When you reach close to full extension of the arms (remember to never lock the joints), you will exhale through the mouth. Do not exhale with the movement, but rather when your arms are close to full extension without locking them. In the beginning, you will move at a moderate rate of speed; not too fast or too slow; simply take your time.

As you inhale through the nose, move the arms down; returning to where you began in front of your forehead. Make certain to inhale with the movement at an even pace.

In the beginning you will breathe at the bottom of all movement concentrating on moving the energy to the palms. In other words, you will breathe out when you get to the apex of the movement. Do this for 10 repetitions.

Pressing Heaven 1   *Pressing Heaven 2*

Pressing Earth

The second exercise in the group is called "Pressing Earth." After you have completed the first set, transition the arms so that your hands are now in front of your solar plexus. This is located about midway down your trunk, where the diaphragm muscle is located. Your thumbs are going to be facing the body with elbows bent. Inhale, and then press the hands down towards the Earth.

Like in Pressing Heaven, do not exhale with the movement just when your arms have almost reached the point of being totally straight. You will exhale from the lower belly through the mouth and focus on the qì moving to the palms of your hands. Move slowly, and do not hyperventilate. Therefore, inhale and bring the hands back up to the starting position in front of the diaphragm/solar plexus. Do this for 10 repetitions.

Pressing Earth 1

Pressing Earth 2

Pressing Heaven and Earth

The third exercise in this group is a combination of the first two exercises and it is called "Pressing Heaven and Earth." One of your arms is going to be moving up and above your head and the other is going to be moving down towards the Earth. It really does not matter which side you choose to start with as you are going to be repeating the same movement on both sides. One set will have your right arm above your head and your left arm at your solar plexus.

You will inhale and when your lungs are full, you will be moving the arms up and down. When you reach that point of almost full extension, you will exhale through your mouth and think about the qì moving from the belly out to the hands. Then inhale through the nose and bring the hands back to the starting position. When you are done with the 10 repetitions with your right hand above and your left hand below you can switch hands. Now do the opposite side; bring the left hand up in front of your forehead and move the right hand down to the solar plexus. Again inhale and then move the arms up and down and when you reach that 90% place of extension you will exhale from the belly, through the mouth.

Originally, when I was taught these exercises I was instructed to watch the movement of the hands, while performing the set. Therefore, do not move your head, but move your eyes, while watching your hands move. Specifically, the eyes look up to Pressing Heaven and look down with Pressing Earth. Consequently, with Pressing Heaven and Earth, I recommend switching eyes; one set I watch the hand go up and the second set I watch the hand that goes down towards the ground.

Pressing Heaven and Earth 1

Pressing Heaven and Earth 2

Pressing Heaven and Earth 3

Pressing Heaven and Earth 4

After you have performed these three nèigōng exercises, you will bring the arms down and place them on your lower belly while you are assuming Wújíbù ("Non-Extremities Stance"), which should be shoulder width apart and the feet facing forward. Make certain to unlock your knees and bend them slightly.

Key Points

Some instructors tell their students to insert their right thumb into the navel, while placing the right hand over the navel, which is followed by having the left hand cupping the right hand. However, if you are the ticklish type; just place your hands over the navel. No need for the thumb in the navel.

Make certain to relax the arms and let them hang down naturally. Also, make certain there is no tension in the shoulders and that the knees are unlocked. Make certain that the tongue is touching the roof of the mouth. Inhale and exhale through the nose throughout the exercise.

You will stand there and breathe for five minutes. Do not set a timer, as you do not want to shock yourself out of the relaxed state you will enter via this form of training with a loud sound. Personally, I use a small clock and watch how much time has elapsed and when I think it is five minutes I stop and take a look. Sometimes I am off the mark, but usually I can tell the lapse of time.

As you stand there breathing you should be visualizing the qì moving up your spine and then falling over your skull and coming down the front of your body in an elliptical pattern of movement. Do not push the qì. Also, do not force or use any tension to move the qì throughout your body. Just relax and visualize the qì moving up and down your body.

With time you will notice that you are able to stand for longer periods. You can spend as much time as you like. The minimum amount of time should be five minutes, but standing for 10 minutes will not hurt you.

In the beginning some individuals are not able to stand for a long period of time. In time a practitioner will develop the stamina to do so, which coincides with striking the Iron Bag. Therefore, these exercises are utilized to assist us in relaxing and as well warming up the body prior to Iron Palm training.

戰鬥鐵
沙掌鐵
衫功協
　會

CHAPTER 4:

THE TOOLS – LINIMENT AND BAGS

Prior to beginning your Iron Palm training you will need to gather some essential equipment. First, you will need a liniment referred to as Dit Da Jáu; second, a training bag; third, the medium you will use within the bag; and finally a stand to place your bag on. Let's look at each in more detail below.

Dit Da Jáu Liniment

The first item you will need to locate and procure is a Chinese liniment referred to as Diēdǎjiǔ within the Mandarin dialect, but better known for its Cantonese pronunciation as Dit Da Jáu. This is extremely crucial component to your training in Iron Skill, because it assists in stimulating blood circulation and reducing pain and swelling, which is ideal for Iron Palm training.

The tradition of Dit Da Jáu stems from the use of various herbs infused in alcohol or other solvents to create a liniment that is used to disperse bruises and stimulate the blood flow. An interesting fact concerning Dit Da Jáu or simply Jáu is that before the discovery of distillation, most liniments were made with rice wine, which possessed a low alcohol count; hence, not very strong. Therefore, people would bury their containers of rice wine and let them sit for long periods of time; allowing the herbs to "marry" and making it potent. However, with the advent of distilling wine into liquor, burying Jáu has become obsolete.

Dit Da Jáu can be typically purchased pre-made via a local Chinese herbal shop or by mail order. However, if an individual would like to produce his own he can; be it by purchasing the individual herbs or buying a pre-made herbal kit to make your own batch of Jáu. However, it is not recommended in the beginning.

Jáu Brewing Method

For those, who would like to make their own Jáu; you should take into account that there are many recipes out there. There are formulas that originated from herbalist and others from martial art instructors, which are traditionally passed down throughout the generation from shīfu to student and are heavily guarded.

Also, there exists different type of formulae for Iron Palm, Iron Body, Iron Arm, and even Iron Finger training, and some are meant for external use only and others can be ingested. Therefore, it is of utmost importance that you make certain you are aware of the function of your formula (i.e., area of the body, or if it is only meant for external use or can it be ingested). If not certain: Do not ingest it, because it can be poisonous! In our case, we are using a general Jáu, which works well in most situations.

Those who would like to make their own brew you will need to acquire the herbs. Below is a formula, which can be taken to a local Chinese herb shop to be filled out. They are also available in a pre-made kit. Once the herbs are in hand you will need to acquire a glass jar, which can contain a gallons worth of liquid, and finally a gallon of grain based alcohol, such as gin, vodka, or whisky.

Now simply add the herbals into the glass jar or a nonmetal container, followed by the solvent (alcohol) of your choice. Typically vodka is preferred and you can purchase the store brand as the value of the vodka does not matter in making your Jáu. Then seal the container and let it sit in a dark and cool place for a stipulated period of time; ideally for six months; the longer the better.

Key Note: Grain based alcohol could easily start a fire or blow up the kitchen, when the alcohol vaporizes and reaches an open flame. Therefore, this heat method uses Rice Cooking Wine as a base for their Jáu, because it is easy to obtain and it contains water, alcohol, and salt, which help to soften the herbs according to traditional Chinese medicine theory.

There are some formulas that required you to cook the herbs prior to making the brew; compared to the first approach, which is referred to as cold soaked. In that case, you do not use grain based alcohol, but Rice Cooking Wine. First heat the solvent and then add the herbs in 30 second intervals and allow it to simmer for 15 minutes.

However, there is a safer method for heating grain based alcohol, which is to heat the bottles in a pan of hot water until the solvent is hot and adding it to the herbs in your specified container. Loosely cover the opening of the container, but do not seal it while it is warm, because this will cause the container to crack or even explode. This has actually happened to me and others, while making a hot soak versus cold soaking herbs.

I personally prefer cooking my herbals for two reasons: One, heating actives the dormant molecules in the herbs, thus making the brew stronger by extracting the rich minerals from the herbs. Second, the fermenting time is decreased from six months down to six weeks. However, I do recommend three or more months of fermenting to make the Jáu potent.

The cold soaked lineaments are just as good as the heated; the big differences between them: One, the fermenting is longer, i.e., six or more months. Second, you can reuse your herbs after using up the Jáu once more. It wouldn't be as potent as your first brew, but still reusable. Thus, at the end it is a personal choice to find a formula that works for you, and assist you in your training.

Therefore, after the mixture has cooled down completely; seal the container and place it in a cool, dark place, where it will age for a stipulated time; six months or more is preferred to make the Jáu the most potent.

Another factor in making Jáu is the decision not to use roughly chopped herbs over grounded herbal powders. However, if you purchase a Jáu kit, this may not be an option. Again, by grinding the herbs down you would increase the surface area, therefore extracting the rich minerals from the herbs. Even if you keep the herbs whole, you will still have a decent product, but it will take longer to extract the active components. However, if you do decide to grind your herbs, be careful as some herbs are fossilized minerals (e.g., bones, resins, or rock-like roots), which can easily break a kitchen grinder. In most cases, for a small fee an herb shop would grind them for you.

After you have made your own Jáu, transfer some of it from the large jar to a smaller container; ideally a cough medicine bottle made out of glass. Make certain to shake up the bottle as some of the residue will gather at the bottom of the container. Then apply the liniment to the area that is being conditioned, rubbing it in until it is absorbed.

Most individuals apply a teaspoon at a time and rub it in until the liquid has been absorbed by the skin, and some use more liniment to lubricate the skin; as they massage the hands, arms, and fingers. However, with palm training, you will rub the Jáu on the heart of the palms, back of the hands, and as well as the knife edge of your hands, before and after training. You can also apply it during the middle of your training session.

Key Note: Never return unused Jáu back into the container because it will contaminate your fresh Jáu. Also, listen to your body. If your hands, arms, legs, or fingers feel sore or stinging from the training, use more liniment.

Here is a very good herbal formula I use for making Jáu. If you can get these ingredients from a Chinese herbal shop or online, great! If not, you can visit my website and either purchase these herbs raw for making yourself, or you can purchase pre-made containers of Jáu for your Iron training. http://www.daledugasherbs.com

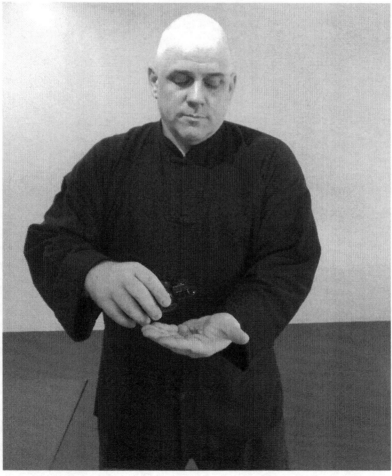

Placing Jáu on the hand

Basic Dit Da Jáu Recipe

1.	海風藤八錢	Hai Feng Teng	24g/Ba Qian
2.	龍膽草四錢	Long Dan Cao	18g/She Qian
3.	細辛三錢	Xi Xin	9g/Sam Qian
4.	續斷八錢	Xu Duan	24g/Ba Qian
5.	歸尾八錢	Gui Wei	24g/ Ba Qian
6.	五加皮八錢	Wu Jia Pi	24g/ Ba Qian
7.	莪術二兩五錢	E Zhu	45g/Yi Liang Wu Qian
8.	三棱二兩五錢	San Leng	45g/ Yi Liang Wu Qian
9.	川楝子四錢	Chuan Lian Zi	18g/She Qian
10.	蛇床子一兩	She Chuang Zi	30g/Yi Liang
11.	川芎八錢	Chuan Xiong	24g/Ba Qian
12.	地榆八錢	Di Yu	24g/Ba Qian
13.	千年健八錢	Qian Nan Jian	24g/Ba Qian
14.	郁金八錢	Yu Jin	24g/Ba Qian
15.	三七一兩	San Qi	30g/Er Liang
16.	柴胡六錢	Chai Hu	18g/Liu Qian
17.	連梗八錢	Lien Geng	24g/Ba Qian
18.	雞血藤一兩	Ji Xue Teng	30g/Er Liang
19.	姜黃八錢	Jiang Huang	24g/Ba Qian
20.	乳香八錢	Ru Xiang	24g/Ba Qian
21.	沒藥八錢	Mo Yao	24g/Ba Qian
22.	威靈仙一兩	Wei Ling Xian	30g/Er Liang
23.	神筋草一兩	Shen Jin Cao	30g/Er Liang
24.	厚朴八錢	Hou Pou	24g/Ba Qian
25.	桑枝一兩	Sang Zhi	30g/Er Liang
26.	地骨皮一兩	Di Gu Pi	30g/Er Liang
27.	寬筋藤一兩六錢	Kuan Jin Teng	48g/Yi Liang Liu Qian
28.	骨碎補六錢	Gu Sui Bu	24g/Ba Qian
29.	烏藥六錢	Wu Yao	18g/Liu Qian

Jáu for Cold Climate Training

If you live in a cold climate or are planning to train outside on a chilly day I encourage the use an herbal soak prior to training. The herbal soak will assist you in warming up the tissues of the hands, allowing blood and qì to flow freely throughout the hand.

Herbal soak formulas usually containing lesser herbs compared to your typical Jáu. The herbs are added to a pot of hot water and allowed to simmer for 10 to 20 minutes over low heat. Make certain that the mixture has cooled down before soaking your hand in it.

Key Note: Most of these formulas are comprised of distinct herbs that are meant to increase the blood and lymph circulation to the hands. Therefore, these particular soaks are great for those individuals who live in a cold climate, because the soak will aid in warming up the hand and lessen the sting of hitting a training bag on those cold and dreary days. Moreover, some soaks are great to use before you break blocks.

Personally, I like to use an inexpensive white wine when making my herbal soaks. For this, take a gallon of inexpensive white wine and add a tablespoon of salt and bring the mixture to a boil. You can also use white cooking wine, which already contain salt. Start placing the herbs into the wine once it has begun to boil. Make certain to turn the heat down to a low simmer and cover the pot. If you do not cover the herbs you will vaporize many of the essential oils and other compounds from the herbs. Therefore, after simmering the soak turn off the heat and allow it to sit for a few minutes and then place your hand in the soak.

Key Note: DO NOT BURN YOURSELF! This is not a contest to see who can withstand burning liquids. Do use common sense; do not harm yourself or your students.

Ideally, soak your hands for five minutes. After soaking, you will rub the liquid into your skin until it is absorbed. You can rub your hands until they are dry, but as long as they are not dripping with

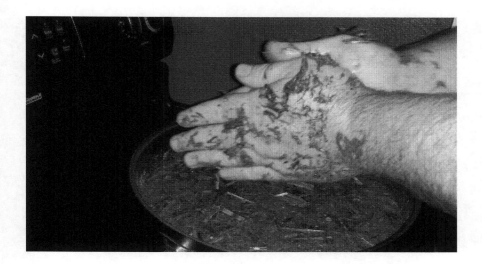

liquid you are good to go. Also, you will not harm yourself if you start hitting the bag with wet hands. However, you will simply be flinging the herbal soak around your training area. Preferably, you want to have more of the liquid absorbed into your skin rather than create a Jackson Pollack painting.

Key Note: When using a soak, there is no need also to use Jáu, because the herb soak consist of the same elements as the standard Jáu. However, you will use your Dit Da Jáu at the end of the session to ensure no injuries. Also, you can store the herb soak by adding a cup of vodka to the liquid before putting it in the refrigerator. You can reheat the solution on the stove in a steel, glass, or ceramic pot, but <u>do not</u> use aluminum cookware, because the impurities found in aluminum would affect the soak. Typically the soak will last a month; just add a cup of vodka each week to ensure that it does not ferment into something other than a usable herbal soak.

Iron Palm Soak Recipe

1.	紅花 六錢	Hung Hua	18g
2.	草烏六錢	Cao Wu	18g
3.	威靈仙八錢	Wei Ling Xian	24g
4.	川烏六錢	Chuan Wu	18g
5.	澤蘭六錢	Ze Lan	18g
6.	桂枝八錢	Gui Zhi	24g
7.	雞血藤六錢	Ji Xue Teng	18g
8.	木瓜六錢	Mu Gua	18g
9.	續斷六錢	Xu Duan	18g
10.	骨碎補六錢	Gu Sui Bu	18g

Striking Bags

You now possess your Jáu; therefore, next on your list is your training bag. It does not matter if you make one yourself or purchase a commercially made bag, which can be found at any local martial art store or mail order supply company.

Training bags can be made from a wide variety of materials, ranging from canvas to leather, but typically they are made of heavy duty canvas, which is durable and economical. The material of the bag is not important, what matters is the strength of the material. A flimsy bag will rip and tear, spilling training medium all over the area.

There are some individuals who make their own bags with or without an inner lining, which is typically a plastic bag to contain the accumulation of the dust that occurs from striking beans or rice.

Also, some individuals use duct tape to cover the striking surface of their bag as an added protection in case the bag tears due to excessive impact it has sustained.

Personally, I do not like to use duct tape or plastic materials for the lining as one can be exposed to toxins from plastic and plastic polymers over time, which is not good. I am cautious; therefore, always err on the side of caution and minimize exposure to anything that could possibly cause harm to my health in the long run. Remember, your healthcare is your own responsibility. Do no harm to yourself or your students with improper training.

Throughout the years, I have made bags from heavy duck canvas as well as denim. However, I now use a custom made bag that is waterproof. It contains a BPA-free waterproof lining within and it is encased in a heavy duty canvas. Because these bags are waterproof, they will not seep out dust, while the bag is being struck.

Another great material for a bag is leather, which is also very good at keeping contact with the medium to a minimum. However, the drawback of leather is the cost. If that is not a problem, I highly recommend it.

Medium - The Bag Fillings

Now you have your training bag, next on the list would be the actual medium (filling) you are going to put into the bag. Typically, most individuals start with some form of beans. Traditionally, a Chinese shīfu would prefer mung beans, because of its availability and cost within their local Chinatown. However, you can use whatever bean

you prefer and even rice can be utilized as a medium. Then, there are some who start off using gravel or metal pellets.

It does not matter which medium you choose per se, but do make certain that it is clean and free from chemicals or contaminants. Ideally, it is better to start off with beans, because it is an easier medium to gauge your progress. In time, the beans will turn to powder, which is a good sign that you are actually progressing in your training. However, be careful when training with a medium that is exposed to air or a bag made of thin material, because you can inhale the dust that comes from the medium breaking down with time.

There are some Iron Skills lineages that talk about inhaling mung bean dust while training. Medically speaking, it does not matter what the medium it is, but inhaling any substances other than air into your lungs over time will cause serious health issues with your lungs. I would rather not risk developing asthma or COPD (Chronic Obstructive Pulmonary Disease) from Iron Skills training; therefore, I do not recommend it.

Then there are some individuals, who train with steel shot or metal pellets, imitating what they have seen in the movies. They strike or rubble their hands within a bucket filled with metal pellets, with or without using liniment prior to training.

However, many who do use liniment are not aware that the liniment assists in absorbing the impurities of the metal pellets into their body, which is not good because the body is absorbing excess iron or impurities into the blood stream. Especially be careful of rust!

Therefore, one has to take into consideration the long term effects certain mediums could have on the body, which is why I personally do not recommend metal pellets due to this inherited risk factor.

Ideally, Iron Palm training should consist of a gradual progression when utilizing mediums. I personally recommend beans or rice in the beginning; due to their availability, cost, and that it is a yielding medium compared to gravel or rocks, which are a solid and coarse medium. Therefore, the first stage of training should be beans or rice, and then followed by gravel or rocks in combination with the use of Dit Da Jáu.

Another key factor besides which medium you utilize is how much to use. I was taught to always have a little room for the medium to move within the bag. Therefore, never fill the bags to 100% capacity, especially in the beginning, when using beans or rice, because you would accidentally assume to do the same when you progress to gravel. Remember, gravel or rocks are hard and do not yield like beans. As such, gravel will need room to adjust to the impact of your palm.

The Bag Stand

At this point, you should have the bag and the medium so now it is time to discuss the need for a stand or table. Make certain that stand/table that you are using is steady and will not move with the first impact, or break over time as a result of continued impact from training.

If you are planning to train outside you can use cinder blocks to make a stand. They are cheap and easy to move. Being 6'2" I use about 6 blocks and two 2x8x16 paver blocks to play with the height of the stand. However, it does not matter which stand you use as long as it is sturdy; you do not want the bag to shift while you are striking it.

The next critical thing about your stand is its height. Actually, the height of the bag is more important than the medium being used, because you do not want the bag to be too high nor too low—both will cause developmental issues later on, which would affect your striking ability. For example, too high of a bag will create a situation where the length of the strike is diminished during the fundamental training.

In the initial stages of Iron Palm training you want to develop a ROM (Range of Motion) that is big and open. Therefore, if you place your bag on a stand too high in the beginning of your training, it can stunt your ability to develop full power at close range, which is one of the objectives in training Iron Palm.

One needs to learn the physical movements and instill them into their muscle memory. After a period of time, training a large ROM will grant the ability to manifest physical power at a certain range, which means that you can now move forward and begin the training to abbreviate that motion/movement into something which is actually being delivered from a shorter distance from the target. This is known as "short power."

When you examine the training methods across different systems, you can see that many place their training bag at or near the same height of the stance they are using. Typically the stance consists of opening up the legs parallel to one another and slightly bending the knees in the Two-Character Stance. Therefore, the height of your stand is correlated to the height of the stance that you are utilizing.

Consider for a moment if you want to practice your Iron Palm in a deep, thighs parallel stance or do you want to be more upright and natural? Personally, I do not like the deep stances as they put way too much stress on the legs and knee joints. Therefore, we have to take into account that this skill is about power development and not harming yourself or causing you to have orthopedic issues in the near future.

With this in mind, the ideal height should be level with the navel or what is referred to as the lower dāntián, as it is believed that qì is developed and stored there and this can be perceived as your body's center of mass.

戰鬥鐵
沙掌鐵
衫功協
會

CHAPTER 5:

IRON SKILLS TRAINING

There are three schools of thoughts when it comes to choosing which hand to develop in Iron Palm training. One school believes that you train your dominant hand, because it is your strongest hand and you want to make it better. Then the second school believes in training the non-dominant hand, because it is weaker and needs to be brought up to par with your dominant hand. And the third school believes in training both hands equally. I suggest that you choose the method that best suits your goals and needs and simply train it. Honestly, no one can determine this for you; only you can. Therefore, contemplate your objective and train accordingly. If the results are not satisfying overtime, simply change your training regimen until you find one to your liking.

Personally, I have trained in multiple methods and feel that there is nothing wrong with having a "strong side" or possessing a "back-up" in your non-dominant hand. However, it is ideal to train both hands to balance one's energy and it is good to be ambidextrous, because you never know what may happen in an altercation.

Training Preliminaries

You went out and purchased your Dit Da Jáu, an Iron Palm Bag containing the medium of choice, and your stand is all set up and ready to use. Now it's time to get down to the actual training program.

Many individuals assume that Iron Skills is an external method due to the overemphasis on hitting the bag. However, that is one small component in the training. The strike is actually the manifestation of the intensive internal training.

In the beginning, you will do the qigong exercises, Standing Post exercises, and the isometric exercises, which will be followed by nèigōng exercises as previously described and shown. All of these are done prior to actually hitting the bag. As such, three-fourths of your Iron Palm training is internal even though the objective seems external.

Once you have completed your warm-ups, you are going to apply your training Jáu to your hands and massage it in until the liquid has been absorbed into the skin. No need to rub it dry, as this can

lead to irritation of the skin. Make certain that you have applied the Jáu to the heart of the palm, the back of the palm, and the fingers. When this is done, you are ready to embark on the striking the Iron Bag.

Penetration and Repetitions

When hitting the bag you are going to tense the hand for about a fraction of a second and then relax. Therefore, do not attempt to strike through the bag or hit it like you are trying to break a cinder block. You should ideally leave your hand on the bag surface for a few seconds.

Key Note: You never want to rush through this process. Slow and steady wins the race, so make certain to relax, breathe in deeply

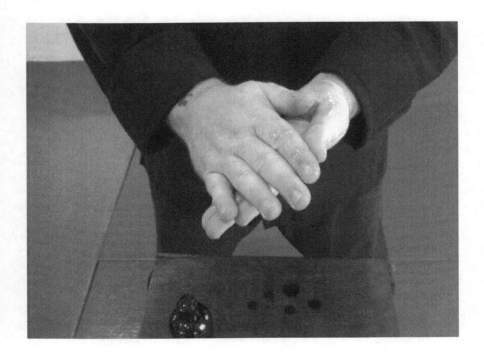

and sense what you are doing. With this in mind, raise your hands to the starting position, which is located in front of the eyebrows. You will do the first three strikes from this position. The last strike is a short strike from a much closer distance compared to the first two strikes.

If you feel a stinging sensation in the hand, you can apply more Jáu and rub it into the hands and then perform some Black Dragon Swings Tail exercises to warm-up the hand once more.

There is no need to rush through your training program. Rushing creates tension and sloppy technique, which is something you want to avoid. Relaxed, steady breathing and letting gravity do its thing will assist you in achieving your goals.

I was taught to strike each of the four areas of the hand for 10 repetitions for the first week of training then adding 10 more repetitions each week until you get to 50 repetitions per hand area. Therefore, try to do 10 repetitions the first week, 20 reps the second week, and so on until you reach the goal of 50 strikes per hand per position. I recommend doing 10 repetitions of Black Dragon Swings Tail between each set of strikes. This will help invigorate the blood and increase circulation within the hand.

Four Striking Method Exercises

You will begin by standing in front of your training bag. In the prior chapter, we mention the height of the bags in relation to your structure. Now let's examine the distance from the bag and yourself. You do not want the bag too close to yourself, because you will not have enough room to move your arm/hand, which will cause problems after a while in terms of straining or absorbing force. Ideally, you want the arms to be relaxed with the elbows bent; not over-extended or curled-up against your body (See corresponding photos).

Personally, I like to place my hand on the bag and then step away from the bag, and play with this until I find the best distance with which my arm is extended and the elbow is not overly bent. Again, the arm and legs should not be stiff so that the joints are open and unlocked, which allows one's qì to flow unobstructed.

Heart of the Palm

Once you have the appropriate distance and the right height, it is time to get down to learning how to strike the bag. Inhale as you raise your arm to eyebrow height, making certain that the hand is open and relax.

The hand should naturally drop onto the bag. Do not exhale until you make contact with the bag. On impact, tense the hand slightly for a second. While exhaling gently squeeze your lower abdomen like it was a bellow and then breathe out in a low hissing breath (making the sound "Ha"). After impact, allow the hand to relax and rest upon the bag for a few seconds, and then inhale and raise your hand once more to eyebrow height and repeat.

Key Note: Make certain to focus on your hand as it raises and that your breathing is in sync with the arm movement. Also, make certain not to move your head; your intent should be on the hand and the bag. Therefore, when the hand reaches the zenith of your

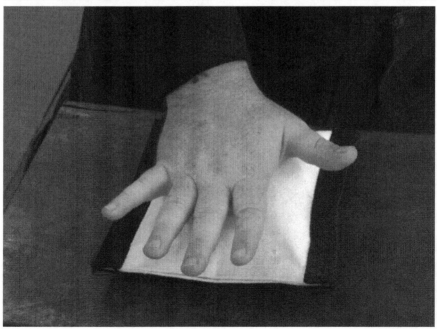

eyebrows, gently rotate the hand so that the heart of the palm is facing downward. You will feel a slight stretch in the hand and then lower your elbow slowly. Do not force this or use too much tension; just make certain to relax the hand and spread the fingers.

Back of the Palm

Now we are going to train the back of the hand, which needs more care than the other anatomical areas because there is less muscle tissue on the dorsal aspect (back side) of the hand, when compared to the ventral section (palm). Caution is required, because the back of the hand can easily be injured while training. For example, the angle it is being dropped can cause a minor issue with the individuals hitting the bones of the wrist, which can be very painful. And getting injured delays one's training time.

As with all strikes performed, you will inhale as you bring the hands up to the ready position. Inhale nice and slow, focusing on your hand rising upwards toward the forehead. When the hand reaches the eyebrows, slowly open your hand wide and rotate the hand so that the heart of the palm is facing downward. Slowly start to drop the elbow first and then as the arm starts to move toward the bag rotate the hand so that the heart of the palm faces up. Make certain to pull the fingers off the bag and hit the flat on the back of your hand against the bag. Exhale when the back of the hand connects to the bag.

Do not breathe out until you make contact with the bag. Tense the hand only for a second and then relax. Allow the hand to remain in the bag for a few seconds. Be conscious of the impact; feel it.

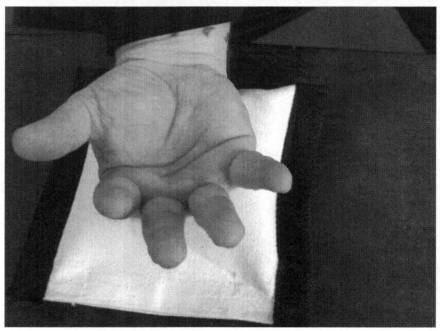

Finally, inhale and bring the hand back up to the starting position in front of your eyebrows, then slowly inhale as you bring the hand/arm back up, watching the movement of the arm with your eyes. When you reached the forehead again, gently open your hand and spread the fingers; pointing the palm away from the body.

Key Note: Do not hurt yourself. If you like you can start out with the arm being closer to the bag, about halfway from the original starting position of the forehead. Over time you will drop the hand from the shorter height and add an inch every week until you can drop the hand from eyebrow height and it does not sting too much or make your hand numb.

Over time the back of the hand will harden and the skin tissues will develop a natural pad, which will protect it from impact. You can use this point as a break in your training to perform Black Dragon Swings Tail, and to apply Jáu for a second time. I was taught to apply Jáu three times throughout my training session: before you start hitting the bag; after training the back of the palm, and when you complete the session.

Key Note: You will minimize injuries by using your Jáu. Therefore, do not be afraid of using more liniment when your hands ache, or if you bruise yourself while hitting the bag too hard. Also, be careful of your training bag. While training the back of the hand, you can create small indentations on the bag; the edge of this indentation when struck with the wrist can be painful. Fluff up your bag often to prevent the indentations from getting too deep. This simple task will reduce the risk of striking an indentation, because you want to make contact with a flat training surface for optimal results.

Outside Edge of the palm

The third striking method exercise employs the outside edge of the palm or the "knife edge," as it is commonly known. This hand area also warrants a little bit of caution when training, especially on gravel or metal shot bag. Along with the back of the palm strike, the knife edge strike when improperly performed can accidentally hit the ring or pinky fingers and/or the tubercle on the outside of the wrist.

Remember that we are training the long bones of the hands not just the finger joints or the knuckles. Therefore, fluff up the bag and pull it over the edge of your stand. This strike is going to be done by changing the angle of the hand as well. You will actually be spreading the fingers and striking the small meaty area just below the knuckle of the pinky to the edge of the hand prior to the wrist.

Inhale as you bring the hand up to the starting position at the eyebrow height. Open the hand and rotate it so that the heart of the palm is facing horizontally and away from the body. Lower the elbow, and strike with the knife edge of the hand on the bag. Exhale when you had made contact with the bag.

As mentioned before, you want to play around with the angle so that you strike the meaty section on the edge of the hand and not your pinky finger or the bones of the wrist. Some individuals like to move in closer to the bag and strike the back edge of the bag away from the front of the stand. Then there are others, who like to squat down a little more and ensure that they are striking the correct area of the hand and not slipping off the stand.

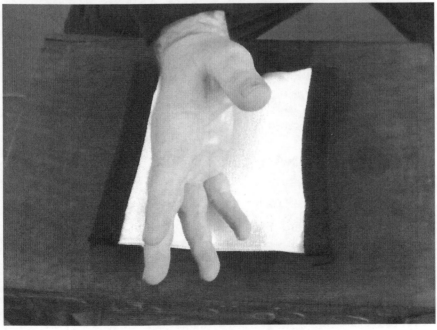

Key Note: You will be making indentations with this strike, but unlike the back of the hand you can strike the edges of the indentations with the edge of your hand; rather like playing a game of "Whack a Mole." You can hit the bag and then on the return strike, come down on the edge of the indentation you created with your previous strike. You do not have to do this per se, but it will not hurt with your progress to have a little fun while training.

Again, listen to your body and do not hurt yourself. Some like to drop the angle of their elbow below the level of the stand and hit the edge of the hand onto the edge of the bag. It does not matter which method you use, but make certain of your safely. As long as you strengthen and condition the area without harming yourself or your students.

Finger Strikes

For iron finger training, I usually teach my students to tap with the fingers and fingertips on the bag using no strength. This is more for the stress to be applied to the fingers in order for them to grow thicker and stronger. There are two methods that one can utilize in conditioning the fingers:

1) Form a Tiger Claw with the fingers by separating the fingers like gripping a jar. With the claw held two inches above the bag, slowly drop the fingers upon the bag; similar to banging a chord on a piano.

2) Form a Crane Beak with the fingers, such that the finger tips are touching one another, as if you were pinching something with all of your fingers. Gently allow the fingers to tap the

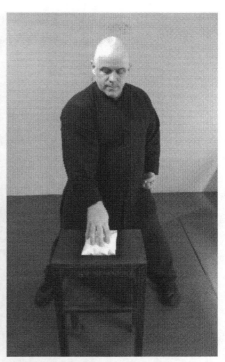
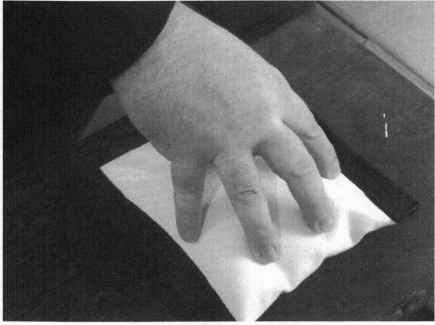

bag. Again, do not use much strength. This is typically done within one or two years of training Iron Palm.

Short Strike

To train short strikes, place your fingers upon the bag and then extend the hand upward by extending the wrist. This is the distance from which you will drop the hand onto the bag. This is more of a stamping or pressing action compared to the slapping method you have done before (i.e., the heart of the palm).

Inhale and bring your hand up to the solar plexus; your bag should be at navel height. Make certain that the hand is relaxed and slowly drop it; at contact spread your fingers as wide as you can. Now slowly lift them off the bag and then strike down your palm. Do not hit the bag hard.

This particular methodology was developed to release short power, or what is referred to as "issuing energy" or Fajin in Mandarin. Therefore, in the beginning you should not inject any penetrating strength into the bag; just drop your hand and allow gravity to do the rest. In time you will learn to inject the right amount of tension at impact. Make certain not to tense up any other part of your body than the hand.

Over time you would develop fajin due to your qìgōng training, which assists you in relaxing your body and increasing your qì, which reinforces the joints, which are crucial in releasing explosive and penetrating energy. Remember: by relaxing, you are increasing your muscle fibers, which then increase your reaction time.

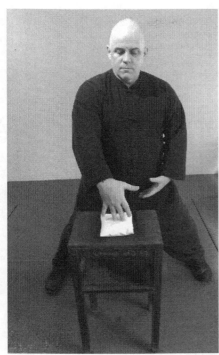

Therefore, with repetitive practice you will notice that your penetrating power has increased greatly.

Key Note: After two years of training you no longer need to execute the strikes from eyebrow level, because you will possess the energy to generate a strike from close-range; hence, no need to wind up to strike.

Brave Tiger Warm Down Exercise

After you are done with the specified number of reps, you will step back away from the bag. At this point you will do an exercise known as "Brave Tiger Scratching Sand." This is a dynamic tension exercise done with a very specific movement and breathing pattern.

First, open up into a horse stance. Next, lift your hands up to your armpits and form a Tiger Claws with your hands, fingers curled in. The position should resemble like someone holding onto a baseball in their hands.

Inhale deeply. When you finish inhaling as much as you can into your lower abdomen, you are going to exhale through the mouth, making a growling or hissing sound, which sounds like "Whaa," while pressing forward with your tiger claws stopping perpendicularly over the knees. At this point tense your entire body for a second and then relax as you inhale and bring the hands up to the starting position right below the armpits.

You will repeat this movement with the breathing three times. On the third execution you will then rub your knees very vigorously.

Getting the hands and the knees warm will assist in increase the absorption of the medicine into your hands.

If you are using a lower stance, this is a good way to increase circulation to the knees and hands after sitting in this stance for a period of time. In the beginning do 10 reps per hand being trained. When you reach the level where you are training for 50 reps per hand per position, for example, you will be sitting in your stance for 45 minutes to an hour depending on the pace of your strikes.

To help healing, rub your hands on your knees for a few minutes and while they are still warm, pour some Jáu and rub it in until absorbed. When you are done, we are going to relax and shake the hands out.

When you are done shaking your hands dry, assume the void stance, while bringing your arms to your sides and slightly behind your hips with the palms facing away from the body. Then you will close your eyes, placing the tongue on the roof of your mouth and imagine that your breath is traveling up your spine; traveling over the top of your head and splitting at the apex of your skull and running down to the arms until it reaches the heart of your palm. Continue standing in this stance and breathing through your nose until you feel the pulsation or heat in the heart of the palm. Once you feel either of these sensations you are finished with your Iron Palm training for the day.

With time and repetition, you will feel a sensation within the heart of your palm. Do not over focus on achieving this sensation; it would occur naturally. Simply allow the qì to flow naturally and in time you will be able to move the energy with your thought. There is a famous maxim: "The Mind Commands; The Body Responds; and the Qì Follows." You will be able to get the qì to flow within your hands, your feet, your elbows, etc. Over time you will be able to move the energy throughout the body.

Foundational Training Period

The "first 100 Days" of training is said to be the magic number needed for one to see results. But actually, after three months and 10 days, one should see an increase in the ability to penetrate with one's strikes; however, this is a not enough time to truly see what can be manifest. Personally, I was taught that the first 100 days serve to set the tone for a more serious training regimen, which should last for two years.

For the first year, you will train the hands twice a day, seven days per week, for 365 days. After this is completed, you would train once a day for the second year. This two year period is considered the foundational training period. Not the 100 days mentioned in many programs. After this two year training program is completed, you can train daily, or you can train a few times a week.

Also, after you complete the two years of training you can then train all your strikes as short strikes on the bag. Over time you will become much more relaxed in all your strikes. When you train enough to inculcate a ROM (Range of Motion) over a few years, you then can abbreviate the movement, but the internal mechanisms are still there, and you will be able to hit as hard as if you moved through the full ROM of that movement.

At this time I personally train 2-3 times per week on average, but there are times when I train more. This training assists me to relax and regain focus. Again, there is no race or finish line to cross. The only opponent you truly have is yourself. Listen to your body, and do no harm to yourself or your students.

Striking Other Objects

Students ask all manner of questions about other Iron Skills training programs that do not employ bags, but solid objects like rocks and metal plates. My Shifu taught me that you want to conceal your skills, and having disfigured knuckles and getting dark skin from hot soaking in certain herbal solutions (like black vinegar), does the opposite of that. It announces to the world that you trained that hand and gives you away as an Iron Palm practitioner.

Personally, I like hitting all manner of objects with my hands as I like to experience the sensation of impact on different substance. I do this to supplement my Iron Palm Bag training. For example, I tap the heart of the palms, the back of palms, and the knife edges of my hands on the trees, walls, and poles as I walk throughout my neighborhood. I do NOT hit them with very much power, nor do I hit my training bags with much power either. For power training, I hit heavy bags, Muay Thai pads or any other training pads that are not stationary and have much more give. Again, do not harm yourself, but hitting your bag too hard.

Bag training gives you great feedback on how hard you are striking. This feedback can help you determine if you are doing something detrimental to your health or if you had properly trained.

For example, I have had a few individuals, which I have personally taught, who had issues with using too much force in their strikes.

Too much stress on your striking arm can lead to stress being absorbed in the chest, which can lead to cardiac issues later on. For instance, the students in question have started to notice irregularities with their heartbeats and chest pain.

After correcting their form and teaching them more exercises to fully gain Sung or relaxation, they fully recovered from their issues. Too much tension can bounce back in your striking arm and lodged within the heart; therefore, hold no tension in your arm and hand until you make contact with the bag, and then the tension are applied only in the hand; do not tense the arm, or the shoulder.

Another dramatic object used in Iron Hand training is a metal plate. Striking metal plates are an advanced form of training, because the plate has no give. At the beginning of one's training one needs to utilize items that have a give due to the risk of injury factor of hitting something solid. Therefore, I only recommend after having some Iron Palm training under your belt and being conscious of how it can affect you.

Again, use your common sense; do not harm your hands by over training on non-moving object. Therefore, if you are training with a metal plate, be aware of the feedback it can give you. Also, remember to use your Dit Da Jáu when training any facet of Iron Palm training.

Pain Mitigation and Management

I receive many calls and emails asking for advice on Iron Skills training and Iron Palm training specifically. Many of these questions fielded to me are concerned the levels of pain and discomfort one may encounter during and after training sessions. Therefore, if your hand is in serious pain; extremely swollen or has become numb from striking the bag; you are doing something wrong.

That is why we use Dit Da Jáu and the herbal soaks, because they assist in protecting your hands and other body parts used during training from experiencing serious injury. Therefore, use the liniment or soak liberally before, during, and after training; also, rest when needed. Again, listen to your body.

If you injure your hand; give the hand a break and do not train through the injury. However, you can do some visualization training instead of physical training. Within your Mind's Eye (as if you are watching a movie of yourself training), picture yourself training the hand on the bags and actually apply Dit Da Jáu onto your hand; liberally until it is absorbed and then visualize yourself training the injured hand in your mind.

Also, many individuals injure the back of their hand early on in their iron skills training because it does not possess the same amount of muscle tissue covering it compared to the palm of the hand.

Over time the tissues on the dorsal aspect of the hand will remodel and thicken. However, be careful when training your hands; the palm is covered with muscle tissue and easily adapts to the striking regimen much quicker than the dorsal portion of the hand. Do not strike your wrist on the bag; there are many small bones in the wrist that can be easily fractured as well as striking joints can lead to early onset of arthritis for people. Remember we are training the long bones in the hand from all sides: Palmar, Dorsal, and Ulnar.

There are systems out there that hit the entire hand on their training bags. I caution anyone to be very careful as the joints are not long bones; they are slightly more complex mechanical systems than a simple bone. Key Note: If you strike the hands flat against a bag; make sure you are not causing harm to the joints of the finger or wrist.

For more detail on herbs for trauma and injury, read Appendix A, which is an in-depth discussion on this topic.

戰鬥鐵沙掌鐵衫功協會

CHAPTER 6:

SLAP STRIKE FOR IRON BODY

By this time you have progressed with your Iron Palm training. However, Iron Palm skills is one component of short-range combat; the other component is referred to as Pāidǎgōng, or "slapping strike achievement" (Pāidǎ, for short). However, these strikes are not meant to be performed on a person, but rather on yourself.

Pāidǎ training is not as complicated as Iron Palm training. For example, you are training the long bones in the arms and legs compared to many small joints and bones within the hands and fingers. Therefore, the objective is to train the osseous tissue as well as the muscle tissues by strengthening them to absorb impact. For that reason, we utilize a program of progressive exercises to condition one's body (e.g., arms, legs, and chest) for impact. Let's consider these below.

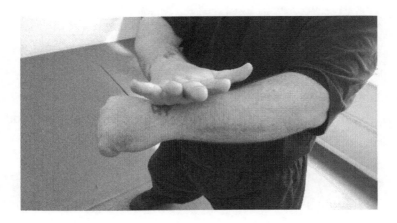

Conditioning the Arms

Let us begin by examining Iron Arm training. A well rounded arm training program should consist of exercises to stimulate muscle and tendon strength, but also bone growth and thickening of the dermal tissue on the arms. This is crucial, because your arms take a lot of abuse when training or applying it in a pugilistic matter or in an actual altercation. Therefore, you want to minimize injuries to yourself and to possibly maximize the ability to cause your aggressor pain.

In most Chinese systems, you will come across some form of Iron Arm routines; using varied methodologies to achieve the goal of arm conditioning. Some of these systems take this training very seriously. In an actual situation you need to possess the ability to absorb an impact, especially when the arm is your first line of defense.

Iron Arm training, is not just about banging your arms with wooden or metal implements or hitting a wooden post or a highly animated training partner. Iron Arm training like other Iron Skills methods is about training the entire body structure; not just a single part.

But before you commence with your Pāidă training, you should perform Standing Post training (as previously mentioned within the qigong chapter) to center the body and the mind and stimulate the circulation of energy within the body. Personally, I like to stand for at least 5-10 minutes; relaxing and simply breathing.

Some methods employ breathing patterns for their arm training, which is a bit different from what we have done before. In this case they like to imagine the entire arm is contracting. The notion is to inhale and imagine that the bones are actually inhaling in air and exhaling carbon dioxide. It is believed that this internal visualization would lead to thicker bones and healthier marrow. If you are curious about this method, attempt it by visualizing that your breathing into the bones of your entire arm and hand.

After completing the Standing Post exercises move on to the Embracing Fist exercises (as described in the qigong chapter.) Start with 10 reps to warm-up the body. After you are sufficiently warmed up, you can begin Pāidǎ training—the most basic of which consists of you slapping your own body.

To begin, start with your arms, slapping from the shoulder all the way down to your fingers by utilizing the whole hand and applying a little power. When you are done with the fingers, hit the bottoms of your palms, then work yourself up the inner forearms until you reach the armpit.

Key Note: Do not hit your armpits with too much power. You can do a few repetitions until you feel the arms getting warm. Also, do not hit yourself to the point of injury. Do stop when you feel any soreness or discomfort; the objective is not to injure yourself.

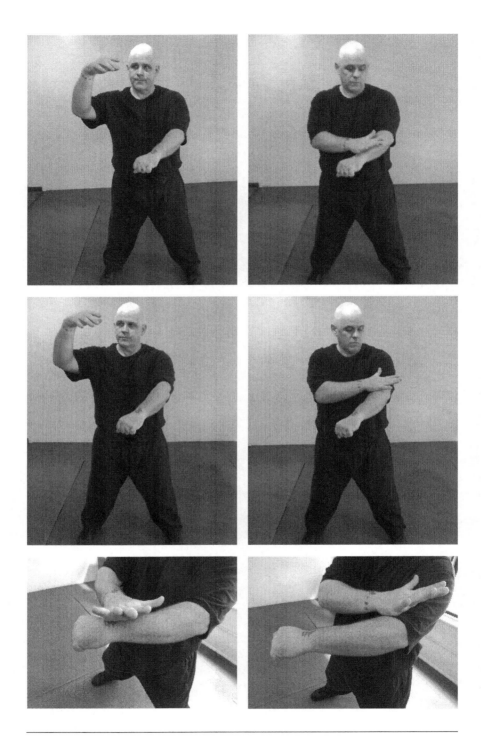

Conditioning the Chest

The easiest way to begin training the tissues of the front of your torso is by opening up to a Two-Character Stance. With knees slightly bent, bring your hands up and rotate your palms so that the heart of the palm is facing towards you. Now relax and inhale. While exhaling sharply, slap your pectoralis (chest) muscles with your hands. Relax and inhale as you bring your hands back to the original position. While exhaling sharply, slap your diaphragm with your hands.

In the same manner and method, strike the entire torso starting with the top of the chest and working your way down to your waist. Do not hit your hip bones due to their hardness. Moreover, be careful not to injure your hand while slapping yourself. Remember to always listen to your body and the feedback it gives you.

Key Note: In the beginning you should not slap yourself very hard. Over time you will train the nerves and tissues to accept more abuse without blinking an eye. Also, if you do get bruised, use your Jáu!

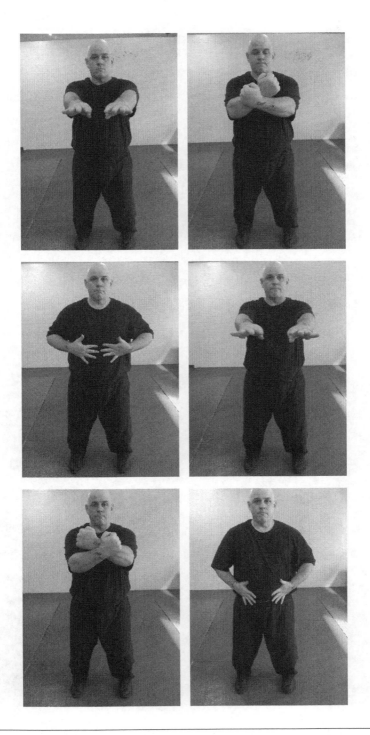

Conditioning the Ribs

After training the chest you can move to the rib area of the torso. Typically, the training consist of striking the Hypochondriac area, which is under the arms and lateral to the chest. Open up to a Two Character Stance. Relax and breathe; while inhaling bring your arms out to their respective sides. Here your arms are wide open and your palms are facing behind you (see accompanying photos). When you cannot inhale any longer, you will pull the arms in very quickly and slap the ribs starting with the area right under your arm. Then you will work down to your waist and back up again. Always inhale and then strike on the exhale. You can use palms or fists to strike yourself. Mix it up, but d not hit yourself too hard and create injury.

Conditioning the Legs

Now let us examine a method to condition the legs. These exercises can be done standing or sitting. The only big difference is that if you choose to stand you are going to be working on your flexibility due to bending over to strike the legs. Here, the exercise is shown sitting.

In the beginning, you will be opening up into a Two-Character Stance, and then inhaling as you bring the hands up to shoulder height with the heart of the palms facing down. When you reach the apex of your inhalation, you will start to relax and slowly drop the arms and begin to slap the front of your legs. Exhale when your hand makes contact with your thighs. Do not breathe out until you make contact with your body. Then, inhale and bring the arms back up to the starting position at shoulder height with your palms facing down. Again, breathe in as slowly and softly as possible while you raise your arms. When you exhale, move to strike yourself, injecting tension into the hands when it makes contact with your leg.

Key Note: Do not tense the hands until you strike the body. Work your way down your legs, around the knees, down to the shins and do not forget your calves. If you like, you can strike the instep and sole of your feet.

You can actually train this while watching TV. Most people will use the palm, but you can also use a fist. Personally, I train with my fists, the back of the hand, and even with a phoenix-eye fist. It really does not matter, which strike you use; just mix it up.

Again with any form of Pāidǎ training; use common sense and do not injure yourself. I recommend the use of Jáu when you are training. Enough cannot be said about not hurting yourself or your students.

Conditioning the Body

The next area of focus is the whole body; therefore, slap the front of your body from the chest then down the thighs and your lower legs to your feet. You can slap the back of your calves, moving up to the back of your thighs, your glutes, your lower back and then bring your hands up and over and slap the upper back and neck as well as gently slapping your head. This will increase overall circulation of blood and lymph, which helps you keep limber; as you have to bend over slightly to train the lower parts of your body.

In the beginning use common sense and do not hit too hard or for too long; eat a healthy and balanced diet and get enough rest. Over time you will see that you will not even blink when you hit yourself.

Using Striking Apparatus

After a period time of hitting oneself with hands, one can move on using some form of apparatus. Traditionally, Chinese Shifu like to start off with a bundle of bamboo chopstick, with which you want to tap up and down the arms and the front of the body. Do not tap the elbows or the kneecaps too hard. You can also tap the head, but remember to be gentle because excessive contact will lead to neurological issues.

From the bundle of bamboo chopstick you can move onto a short wooden stick to train the arms. Start with tapping the top side of the arm and moving down the arm and then hitting the underside of the arm as they go up the arm toward the shoulder. Do not strike with the stick on the bones of the wrist, the elbow joints, or the armpits very hard. There are too many nerves plexus located there.

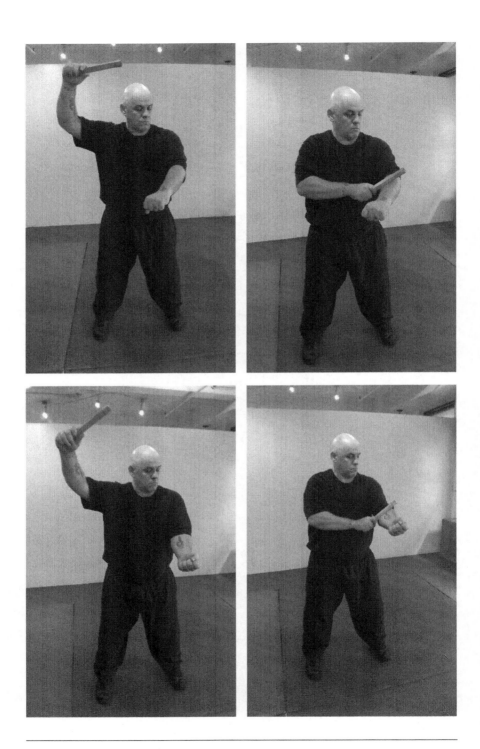

Another method is to roll the stick on the forearms, upper arms and shoulders.

After you been tapping your arms for a while and feel inclined to move forward to an advanced level. You can purchase Iron Body Sack or a metal wire hitter.

Key Note: It does not actually matter which apparatus you use. What counts is to stick to a training regimen and track your progress. Therefore, take notes and keep a log of your reps and what tools you are using, how many days per week you are training the arms, etc.

Make certain to start off slow and listen to your body; make sure you are using Jáu while training with the wire hitter. Therefore, tap your arms as you did with the wooden stick, tapping the tissues and long bones of the forearm, the upper arms and shoulders. Do not hit the shoulder joint bones nor any other joints or obtruding tubercles.

Pāidǎ training offers a sense of security for those that pursue a pugilist activity. It does not matter if it is in the ring or the street, because you are conscious of the limitation of your body; whereas others, who do not practice pāidǎ are not certain if their body can absorb a blow or not. Therefore, pāidǎ is a crucial component in a pugilistic pursuit.

CHAPTER 7:

BREAKING OBJECTS

When you have trained your hands for at least two years or more, you can take your Iron Palm training to the next level by breaking objects. Breaking is a pressure gauge to test one's conditioning and penetrating ability. Lets' look at a few different mediums you can use for breaking and testing your Iron Skills.

Wood

Usually wooden boards are the first medium utilized in the art of breaking. I recommend beginning with one-inch thick dry pine boards free from huge knots. They are relatively inexpensive, easy to obtain and easier to break compared to bricks or blocks. You can also try out the many re-breakable boards available at local martial arts supply stores or online companies.

Breaking is not just about going nuts and winding up and throwing your arm at a stack of something. There is a method to the madness. You want to set up the boards between two cinder blocks (stanchions), which are set to your height. I like to place the boards at mid-thigh level. For a stand I recommend cinder blocks and paving blocks to ensure the height of the stanchions is spot on. Refer to Chapter 5 for more on this.

Before breaking any object it is best to warm up the hands to increase blood flow and qi, so as to reduce chances of injury.

In the beginning, start with one board; use the heart of the palm strike first. After attaining this skill attempt breaking a board with the back of your hand. Follow this with the knife edge. After feeling comfortable with these achievements, move on to breaking two boards, and so on.

After breaking three boards some individuals will use very thin spacers as they stack on a greater number of boards. Be sure not to use anything bigger or thicker than a standard No.2 pencil. Once you can break multiple boards easily with spacers, you then can start removing the spacers. Start at the top of your stack and work down to the bottom. Eventually, you will be able to break a stack of boards without the assistances of spacers.

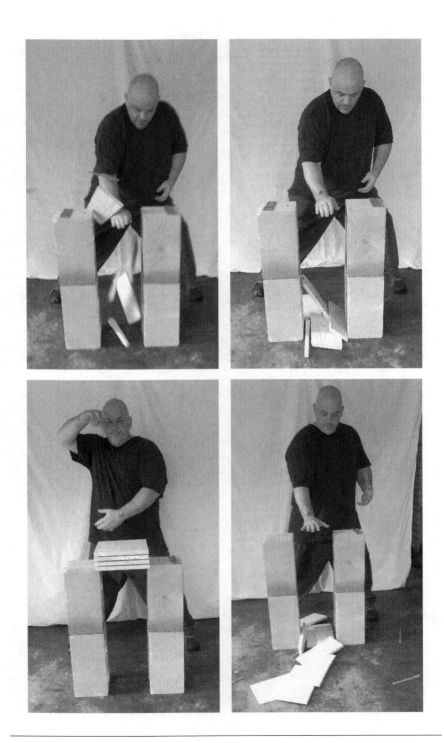

Paving Blocks

After wooden boards most people graduate to the next breaking medium, which is paving blocks. They are harder than wood and so are a good gauge of one's progress. Just like before, make sure the height of the blocks is in proportion to your height. Also, I suggest using an old washcloth to cover the area of the block where you will be hitting. I recommend this from my personal experience of getting cut on the jagged edges of the concrete blocks as they break under my strikes.

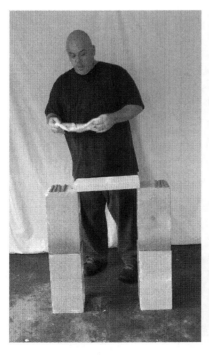

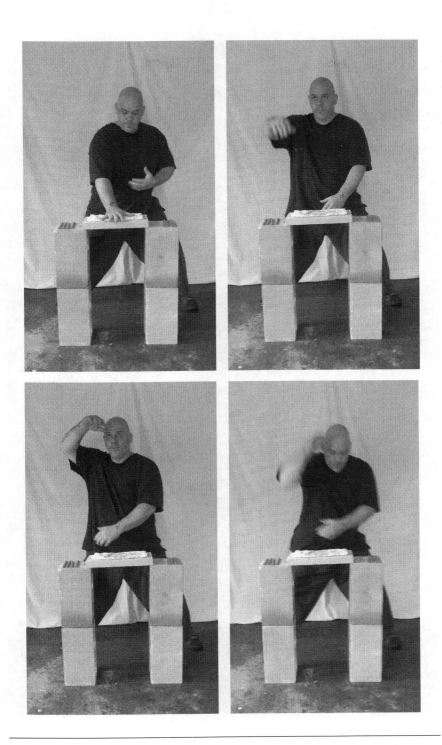

As with boards, you can start to use spacers. Most individuals will use spacers on a stack of eight blocks or more. In time you can start to remove the spacers, starting at the top of the stack and working down to the bottom.

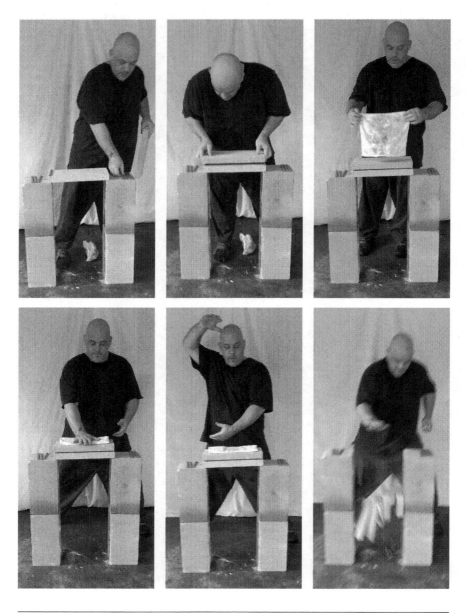

In addition to the heart of the palm and the knife edge, you can also break with the back of the hand. It is done in the same way, using spacers for multiple paving blocks and a towel overtop so as not to cut your hand.

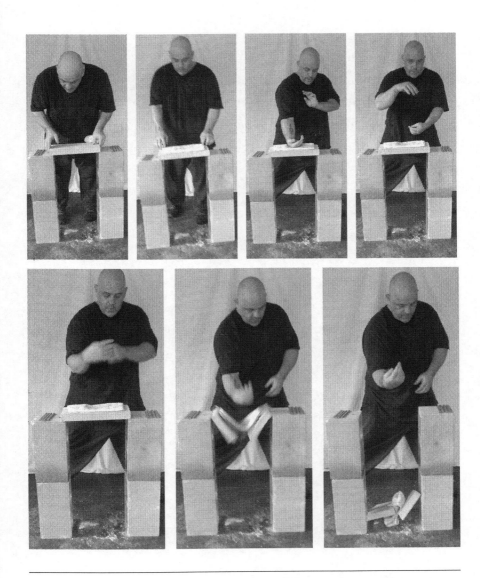

Key Note: Be extremely careful as it is very easy to injure yourself when you are attempting breaks, especially with bricks and blocks. Throughout the years, I have dealt with a few students getting injured and needing my acupuncture skills in their recovery.

Advanced Breaking

Once you have tried and succeeded in breaking boards and blocks and are still training your Iron Palm, you can move on to what people may term as advance breaking. For some, this implies breaking unusual items. For example, I like to use coconuts at this stage. They are hard to break and will give you all manner of interesting stories to tell others.

Start with a coconut and place it onto the ground, or on a stanchion. There is a seam on the coconut, which is a good place to strike it. Once you can break a coconut in this way, you can attempt to break a coconut held in your hands or on a suspended bag. This particular feat will take your breaking ability to another level due to the speed and power needed to break a non-stable and unsupported object; hence, a new plateau to strive for.

The hardest breaks are the ones where you are only breaking one brick or block out of the respective stack. Most people train to try and make the bottom brick break first, which is not that easy to do. Others try and break the top brick on the stack, while others attempt to break a brick or block in the middle of the stack.

Breaking is a great method to gauge one's conditioning and ability to penetrate and inject power into a target. I like breaking, because it teaches one how to apply power without harming one's training partners.

戰鬥鐵沙掌鐵衫功協會

CHAPTER 8:

SCATTER HANDS –
IRON SKILLS APPLICATIONS

Once you have trained your Iron Skills for a sufficient period of time, you will possess the hands and the body to deliver powerful strikes and absorb major impact, which are crucial elements for a pugilist.

You now possess hands that are conditioned and powerful, which can be utilized to strike various pressure points on the human body. Let's examine some of the easily accessible pressure points; starting with those on the head, which can be struck to the heart of the palm.

Personally, my objective is to penetrate with my strikes; not just to tap my opponent. As a result, the fighting methodology I use is referred to as "shorthand," because I engage and opponent at distance shorter than two feet. I block or intercept an incoming attack and counter with a penetrating strike.

Vital Points

Let us examine some acupuncture points that are easy to recognize and strike. For example, acupuncture points Stomach 1, 2, 3, and 4 are located on the front of the face starting from under the eyes. These points run in a line from under the eye and down the cheek traveling to the mandible where the acupuncture channel then travels up the mandible to pass in front of the ear and up to the corner

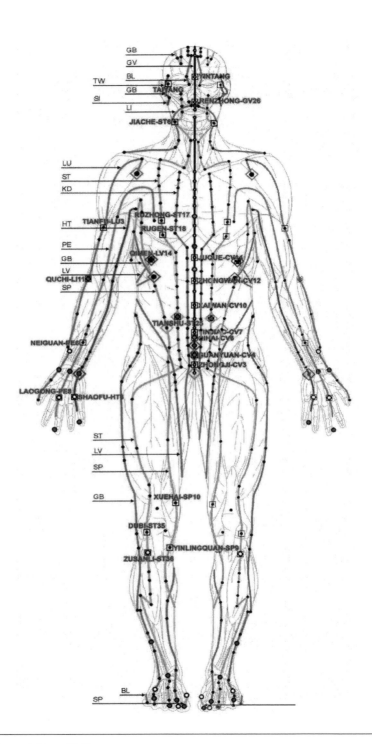

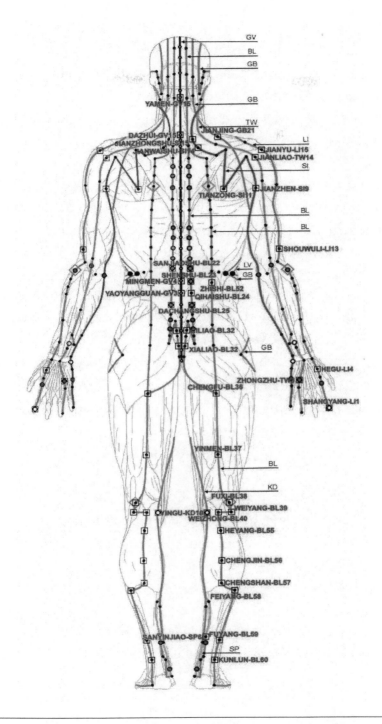

GV
BL
GB

GB

TW

JIANJING-GB21

LI

YAMEN-GV15

DAZHUI-GV15
JIANZHONGSHU-SI15
JIANWAISHU-SI14

JIANYU-LI15
JIANLIAO-TW14

SI

TIANZONG-SI11

JIANZHEN-SI9

BL

BL

SHOUWULI-LI13

SANJIAOSHU-BL22
SHENSHU-BL23
MINGMEN-GV4
ZHISHI-BL52
YAOYANGGUAN-GV3
QIHAISHU-BL24

LV
GB

DACHANGSHU-BL25

SHANGLIAO-BL32
XIALIAO-BL32

GB

ZHONGZHU-TW3

HEGU-LI4

CHENGFU-BL36

SHANGYANG-LI1

YINMEN-BL37

BL

KD

FUXI-BL38
WEIYANG-BL39
YINGU-KD10
WEIZHONG-BL40

HEYANG-BL55

CHENGJIN-BL56

CHENGSHAN-BL57

FEIYANG-BL58

SANYINJIAO-SP6
FUYANG-BL59

SP

KUNLUN-BL60

of the head where the side of the skull meets the front of the skull. This makes all of these points ideal for striking with one's palm or the knife edge of the hand as well as with the hammer fist. The points on the mandible include Stomach 5 and 6. The point in front of the ear is Stomach 7 and the pressure point on the edge of the skull is Stomach 8.

Other points on the skull in the temporal region are also easily targeted and struck, including Gallbladder 1, which is right next to the eyes, along with Gallbladder 2 and 3 which are located in front of the ear as well.

There are many points along the entire arm which can be struck as well. Where your arm meets your torso contains both Lung 1 and Lung 2. When struck with power, one can cause the breathing to be negatively affected. Points on the lower arm include Large Intestine 10 and 11, which are located near the elbows. Striking these points can cause numbness and pain immediately. Most of these points are struck in combination. The torso and arm points are attacked using the arms while your legs can attack points on the lower body.

Let us next examine pressure points that are located on the torso and the legs. The area of the torso where the ribs branch out from the trunk is a well-known place to strike if needed. The point where the ribs begin to branch off the side of the body is Liver 13, which is a great point to strike with hands, elbows, and even knees.

Upper leg points include Gallbladder 31, which is located on the lateral side of the thigh in the middle of the thigh. This is a great point to strike which will cause "jelly leg" syndrome. You kick or strike this point and the leg will go numb, hence the term jelly leg.

Gallbladder 34 is a lower leg point located below the knee joint, along the lateral portion of the lower leg; along with Stomach 36 which is located more medial than Gallbladder 34. Both of these points are great targets to help cut the foundation out from under your opponent using, for example, an Iron Broom sweep attack to these points.

Personally, I like either slapping or kicking these points with either a downward or sideways trajectory using the palms, fists, or fingers. When you strike the head, the energy and momentum inserted into the skull causes a temporary neurological shutdown within the brain and Central Nervous System (CNS). One of my shifu referred to this as "brain blinking," as the brain attempts to deal with an overload of physical energy that was delivered via the striking of Stomach 1-4 on the face. When struck in the head or face, most will close their eyes. Once they shut their eyes, you can then ramp up the response to their attacks as they are not in a very advantageous position and their balance has been affected negatively.

Some individuals will even strike at the opponent's eyes by employing the back of the palm, which is referred to as Floating Palm or as some call it, "Beauty Looks into the Mirror." Allow your fingers to relax and then fling your entire hand at the target. You can also utilize finger tips and strike the eye socket themselves. As you can see, your training is only limited by your own imagination and martial arts material.

Another acupuncture point, Governing Vessel 20, known as Bai Hui, which is located at the vertex of the skull. This particular point along with the entire occipital area of the head and the temporal region of the skull are ideal target areas to strike. Therefore, palm strikes onto the skull should not be a problem for someone who has trained their hands. However, be careful with using the back of the palm, which does not have enough muscle to protect the bones and tendons, when striking the skull or other bony hard areas.

With the acquisition of Iron Palm and Iron Body skills, you will become a formidable opponent. Understanding basic human anatomy and physiology and the names and locations of acupuncture points, will make you even better. Iron Body will grant you the ability to absorb physical attacks and not blink or pause as an untrained person will do.

Iron Palm Fighting Applications

Technique 1: Baguazhang – Eight Trigram Palm

The author intercepting an incoming Level Strike (平吹) with a Piercing Palm (插掌). The initial Piercing Palm converts to Seizing Hand (捋手), which allows him to have control of the assailant. At which point the author executes a Covering Palm (盖掌), which is followed by a Knee Press (膝压) into the back of his assailant's knee. While still holding onto the assailant's wrist the authors sweeps back the lead arm, executing a Hooking Leg (勾腿) to the assailant's leg. The assailant falls.

Technique 2: Baguazhang – Eight Trigram Palm

The author intercepting a Sweeping Strike (扫吹) with a right Detain Hand (扣手). The Right Hand converts to a Seizing Hand, while executing a Covering Palm to the opponent's rib cage. However, the opponent executes a Piercing Strike (贯吹), which the author counters with Wing Arm (膀手). Now the author's left arm converts to a Swing Arm with the intent to embrace his opponent to off leverage him. Finial the author executes an Embracing Waist, Crossing Back (抱腰过背). The opponent hits the ground.

Technique 3: Baguazhang – Eight Trigram Palm

The opponent throws a Horizontal Swing Leg (橫擺腿). The Author executes an Embracing Arm (抱手) to scoops the opponent's leg. The Author now executes a Swing Palm to the opponent's knee. Now the Author twist the opponent's leg, which hurls him towards the ground. The opponent hits the ground.

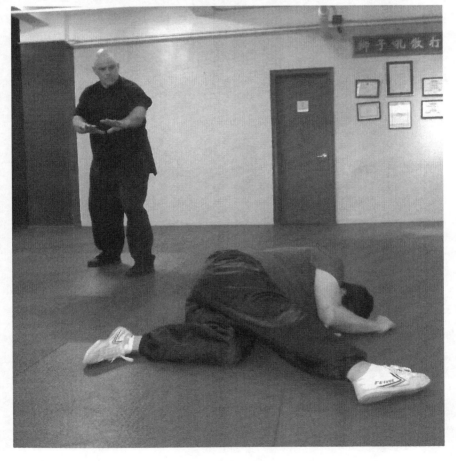

Technique 4: Kwang Sai Jook Lum – Southern Mantis

The Author Stands on Guard (防). The opponent throws a Level Strike, which is interceptive with a Seizing Hand. The Author now executes a Pressing Palm (按掌) to the opponent's face. The opponent's response with a Sweeping Strike, which the Author intercepts with a Detain Hand. The Author starts to execute a Throwing Elbow (撇肘) technique. Now the Author finalize the Throwing Elbow technique. The opponent falls The Author quickly respond with Planting Strike (栽吹).

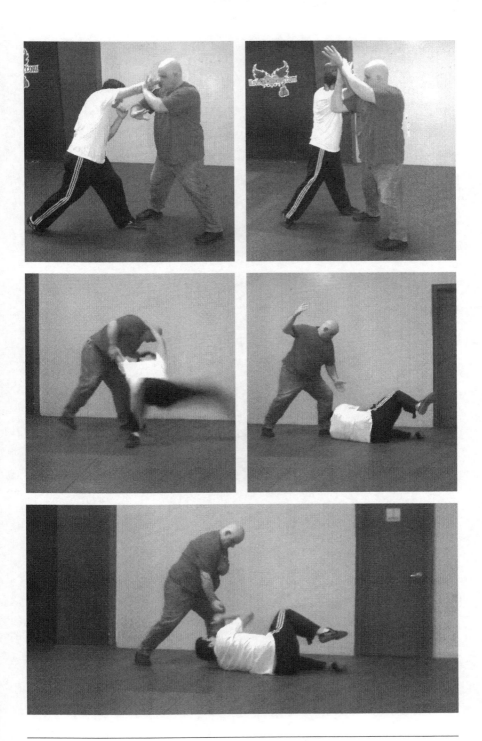

Technique 5: Kwang Sai Jook Lum – Southern Mantis

The opponent starts to throw a Horizontal Swing Leg to the Author's thigh. The Author quickly block the incoming kick raised knee. The Author now moves in with a Positive Palm (阳掌) to the Opponent's face. Now the Author press down on the head, while lifting his the opponent's arm to unbalance him. The head press converts to an actual throw. The opponent falls.

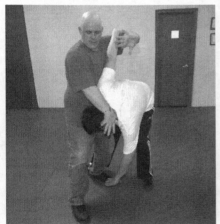

戰鬥鐵沙掌鐵衫功協會

AFTERWORD:

THE BEGINNING

Iron Skills were developed for a harsh reality, when one's body was one's weapon. However, this day and age is not as harsh as when the elders devised these unique methods to forge the human body into iron.

Even though Iron Skills grant a pugilist a sound method to condition the body—be it for sport as a competitive fighter or for the harsh reality of that the streets may offer—its true benefit is actually health; not violence as some may believe. It goes beyond the obvious, which is a physicality, into something deeper, which benefits our health tremendously. Who would believe breaking a coconut would do that?

In Chapter One, we were introduced to the roots of Iron Skills within the United States of America. This chapter emerged as a reminder of the individuals that broke the code of silence and decided to share this ancient knowledge to an eager audience, and hopefully this book inspires others to treasure and preserve these methods for another century.

In Chapter Two I was able to share the significance of Iron Skill, which is the science behind forging one's body. And in Chapter Three went deep in the alchemy of Iron Skills, which is Qìgōng.

Qìgōng is a complex notion which allows us to become one with ourselves. It is a conversation with our psyche, which is as crucial in today's society as it was for the battlefield of yesteryears, but at the same time improves our body. Without those two core notions you cannot have Iron Skills. Indeed, something so physical is in reality, something so intangible.

In Chapter Four we examined the tools you need to forge your body and by Chapter Five we enter that secret room and start to forge the body as it was depicted within those kung-fu movies of yesteryear.

Chapter Six allows us to gauge our progress with different mediums, which should bring a smile to one's face, as seeing one's progress is so rewarding. That is why I introduce this methodology in a step-by-step process to grant the practitioner the ability to gauge his progress. Remember, there are no shortcuts when one's heart is involved.

In Chapter Seven we venture beyond the hand and started to focus on tempering the body for impact. At times, some individuals forget that fighting is not like in the movies; no wires, but up and close. Very personal, which means you would get hit; therefore, one's body needs to be able to absorb impact.

Finally, in Chapter Eight, we tied it all in to demonstrate why we train Iron Skill, which is to be able to survive an encounter when needed.

In closing, this is the beginning of one's journey in exploring oneself and what we are able to do if we focus our intent into forging our body into Iron. Enjoy the process, train hard, and heal fast.

—Dr. Dale Dugas
www.DaleDugas.com

APPENDIX A

Chinese Medicine for Physical Injuries

An Interview with Dr. Dale Dugas by Dr. Mark Wiley

Every day people experience pain and physical injury from simple things. You can develop a stiff neck from sleeping wrong or a twisted ankle from a wrong step in sports or suffer broken bones from accidents.

Many of these – what I call "ordinary life pains and strains" – are not serious and do not require serious medical attention. But when left untreated, or if treated improperly, they can become chronic. One of the best overall modalities I have found to work well for many forms of physical trauma (e.g., pain, inflammation, bruising and strains) is traditional Chinese medicine (TCM). This is especially the case when undertaking hard training in the martial arts, especially in the methods of iron skills as depicted in this book.

TCM dates back thousands of years and has many different modalities that it uses to treat different forms of physical trauma. My friend and colleague, Dr. Dale Dugas, specializes in making herbal formula, teas, and topical liniments for physical trauma and I asked Dale what he thought the best forms of TCM were for treating physical injury. I thought I'd share his thoughts with you here to help you complete your understanding of true martial skills: harm and heal.

What are some of the different ways in which TCM treats trauma?

"Acute injuries typically manifest with moderate to severe pain, swelling, redness and heat. This is usually localized in the area that has been injured. External herbs can be applied to help reduce inflammation, decrease swelling and help deal with pain. These herbs are usually "cooling" and "moving" in their nature. You can prepare an oil based balm/paste with these herbs. They are applied to the injured area and covered with gauze and used for the first 24 hours to help reduce pain and swelling. Internal herbs (whether in raw form or prepared as pills/capsules), can be used to help deal with the swelling and pain caused by the trauma."

"Other practitioners use a medicated plaster, which has herbs processed into the adhesive. These plasters are then applied to the affected area, and typically will be left on for three to 12 hours. The herbs in the adhesive help to reduce pain, increase circulation and help with increasing the blood flow to the injured area. Usually these types of plasters are used after the initially swelling has decreased."

"Herbal liniments called *Dit Da Jáu* (literally, Fall Strike Alcohol) are also used. The liquid made from herbs steeped into alcohol is applied to the area affected. Formulas with cooling herbs can be used to help reduce the initial swelling of an acute injury, but usually liniments are used in a manner similar to applying and using a plaster—i.e., after the swelling has decreased would this modality be used on an injury."

What are some of the "hands on" treatment methods used?

"Acupuncture points can be stimulated with needles or finger pressure to help reduce swelling, pain and increase blood circulation in the area affected. Tuīná is a form of therapeutic massage that is used in TCM. After the swelling has decreased, medicated oil can be used to help increase blood circulation as well as a skin lubricant, and the affected area is worked on to help increase blood circulation as well as work out the fluids that have collected there due to the initial swelling from the injury."

How does a TCM practitioner decide which method(s) to utilize in the healing process?

"Depending on the severity of the injury and the amount of heat and swelling at the affected area, most practitioners agree that one has to deal with the heat, pain and swelling immediately. Modern use of ice was not utilized in China, as many would say the use of "ice was for dead people.""

This is a big difference with Western thinking.

"Right and so herbs and balms/plasters can be applied quickly and easily, in or outside of a TCM clinic. These can easily be carried around in a first aid kit. Some TCM practitioners will bleed distal acupuncture points to affect an immediate healing response to an acute injury."

Sure, but this should only be done in a sterile setting, and not by a person looking for self-care.

"Right, and the usual situation is that people do not come into TCM clinics with acute injuries, they come in after the initial 24-48 hour period and have mild to moderate swelling and an increase in pain. If the initial heat and swelling has been reduced, we start to work on increasing blood circulation in the affected area. Warming and pain-reducing herbs/liniments can be used to help increase blood flow."

What about chronic injuries?

"Chronic injuries can be stubborn as they have been around for a period of time. One could use a hot external liniment or a strong internal formula to help increase blood flow, help open the acupuncture channels and reduce pain."

In your experience, what are some of the most-used herbs for different forms of physical injury, or trauma?

"Inflammation: Bo He(mint), Chuan Xiong (Lovage Root), Mu Dan Pi (Peony Tree Root Bark), Ru Xiang (Frankincense), Bai Zhi (Angelica Root)."

"Pain: Yan Hu Sou (Corydalis Root), Bai Shao (Peony Root), Bai Zhi (Angelica Root), Chai Hu (Buplerum root), Hai Feng Teng (Kadsura Pepper Stem), Mo Yao (Myrrh)."

"Bruising: Chi Shao (Red Peony Root), Dang Gui Wei (Chinese Angelica Root), Hong Hua (Safflower)."

"Tendonitis: Xu Duan (Dipsacus Root), Mu Gua (Chinese Quince Fruit), Shen Jin Cao (Clubmoss)."

What are the pros and cons of using plasters, Dit Da Jáu and herbal pills?

"The biggest benefit using trauma plasters are their ease of use. They are like bandages: You can store them anywhere. All you have to do is peel off the backing and stick them over the injury site. The only drawback is for people that are hairy. Removal could be a little painful and you will lose some body hair in the process. Dit Da Jáu Liniments are great in that you will not lose body hair. The liquid is applied and rubbed into the injury site until it is fully absorbed dermally. The liquids can stain clothing so be careful. Some liniments are very odiferous and your co-workers might think you own a spice house. Patent medicines are herbs that are ground and pressed into tablets and rolled into tiny round pills. They are easy to store and have on your person or in your first aid kit. The only drawback is you have to ingest the pills and then digest them and then have your body figure out what to do once your body has recognized the herbs. Also if you drop the pills on the floor, they are like tiny ball bearings and will roll and disappear under furniture etc."

It seems like using the Dit Da Jáu liniment is safe and easy. Can one make their own?

"Making a basic Jáu liniment is easy. You can take Hung Hua (Safflower) 18 grams, Ru Xiang (Frankincense), Mo Yao (Myrrh) both 18 grams, Xu Duan (Dipsacus Root) 18 grams, and Shen Jin Cao (Clubmoss) 18 grams and add this to a half gallon up to a gallon of Vodka in a glass container. Do not waste your money on high end alcohol; store brand vodka is perfectly fine. Add these herbs whether whole or cut up into big chunks into the medium. You can agitate it daily for one week and place the glass container in a cool and dark place. Most people put it in the garage, basement or closet. You want the herbs to be covered and not exposed to light, as well as cool and dry. Let this sit for six weeks and you can then decant some into a smaller container and begin to use it. Apply it to injuries after the initial swelling has gone done. Or you can purchase pre-made bottles from various suppliers."

Thank for all the pointers, Dale! Where can one learn more about TCM for trauma and even ask you questions directly?

"They can visit my website www.daledugas.com for more information, or come see me at any of the clinics I work out of in the Tampa, FL area. Let me know how I can be of service."

APPENDIX B

Terminology - English and Chinese with Characters

(As terms appear in each chapter)

Introduction

English	Pinyin (Mandarin)	Yale (Cantonese)	Simplified	Traditional
Iron Skill	Tiějì	Tit Geih	铁技	鐵技
Iron Palm	Tiězhǎng	Tit Jeúng	铁掌	鐵掌
White Eyebrow	Báiméi	Baahk Méih	白眉	白眉
Heaven Descending Order	Tiānxiàdìyīquán	Tín Hah Daih Yàt Kyùhn	天下第一拳	天下第一拳
Iron Body	Tiěshēn	Tit Sàn	铁身	鐵身

Chapter 1: Brief History

English	Pinyin (Mandarin)	Yale (Cantonese)	Simplified	Traditional
Ruzhang Gu	Gù, Rǔzhāng	Gu, Yúh Jeùng	顾汝章	顧汝章
Southern Capital	Nánjīng	Naahm Gìng	南京	南京
The First National Guóshù Exam	Dìyī-jièguóshùkǎo	Daih Yàt Gaai Gwok Seuht Háau	第一届国术国考	第一届國術國考
Yibing Xu	Xú, Yībīng	Chèuih, Yàt Bìng	徐一冰	徐一冰
Tieshang Chen	Chén, Tiěshēng	Chàhn, Tit Sàng	陈铁生	陳鐵生

English	Pinyin (Mandarin)	Yale (Cantonese)	Simplified	Traditional
Zhijiang Zhang	Zhāng, Zhījiāng	Jeùng, Jì Gòng	张之江	張之江
Spirit Martial	Jīngwǔ	Jìng Móuh	精武	精武
Bruce Lee	Lǐ, Xiǎolóng	Léih, Siú Lùhng	李小龙	李小龍
Spirit Martial Gate	Jīngwǔmén	Jìng Móuh Mùhn	精武门	精武門
Jet Lee	Lǐ, Liánjié	Léih, Lihn Giht	李连杰	李連傑
	Jīngwǔyīngxióng	Jìng Móuh	精武英雄	精武英雄
Country	Guóshù	Gwok Seuht	国术	國術
Striking Platform (Ring)	Lèitái	Leùih Tòih	擂台	擂台銳
Young Forest Five Family Fist	Shàolínwǔjiāquán	Siu Làhm Ngh Gà Kyùhn	少林五家拳	少林五家拳
Ark Yuey Wong	Huáng, Déruì	Wòng, Dàk Yeuih	黄德锐	黄德
Martial Establishment	Wǔguǎn	Móuh Gwún	武馆	武館
Chinese Emigrant	Huáqiáo	Wáh Kiùh	华侨	華僑
Tim Yuen (T.Y.)Wong	Huáng, Tiānyuán	Wòng, Tim Yùhn	黄添源	黄添源
Young Forest Buddha Family Fist	Shàolínfójiāquán	Siu Làhm Faht Gà Kyùhn	少林佛家拳	少林佛家拳
Sincere Citizens	Qiánmín	Kihn Màhn	虔民	虔民
James Yim Lee	Yán, Jìnghǎi	Yim, Geng Hói	严镜海	嚴鏡海
Buddhabhadra	Bátuó	Baht Tòh	跋陀	跋陀

Chapter 2: Overview of Iron Palm Training

English	Pinyin (Mandarin)	Yale (Cantonese)	Simplified	Traditional
Palm	Zhǎng	Jeúng	掌	掌
Palm Heart	Zhǎngxīn	Jeúng Sàm	掌心	掌心
Palm Root	Zhǎnggēn.	Jeúng Gàn	掌根	掌根
Palm Back	Zhǎngbēi	Jeúng Bui	掌背	掌背
Palm Outside Along	Zhǎngwàiyán,	Jeúng Ngoih Yùhn	掌外沿	掌外沿
Back Knife	Bèidāo	Bui Doù	背刀	背刀
Palm Finger	Zhǎngzhǐ	Jeúng Ji	掌指	掌指

Chapter 3: Internal Training Exercises

English	Pinyin (Mandarin)	Yale (Cantonese)	Simplified	Traditional
Air Achievement	Qìgōng	Hei Gùng	气功	氣功
Air	Qì	Hei	气	氣
Standing Post	Zhànzhuāng	Jaahm Jong	站桩	站椿
Everlasting Post	Wújízhuāng	Moùh Gihk Jong	无极椿	無極椿
Two character Stance	Èrzìbù	Yih Jih Bouh	二字步	二字步
Propping-Up, Embracing Post	Chēng-bāozhuāng	Chaang Póuh Jong	撑抱椿	撑抱椿
Hundred Gathering	Bǎihuì	Baak Wuih	百会	百會
Gathering Overcast (Perineum)	Huiyin	Wuih Yam	会阴	會陰
Cinnabar Field	Dāntián	Daàn Tihn	丹田	丹田

English	Pinyin (Mandarin)	Yale (Cantonese)	Simplified	Traditional
Outside Achievement	Wàigōng	Ngoih Gùng	外功	外功
Horse Stance	Mǎbù.	Máh Bouh	马步	馬步
Embracing Fist	Bàoquán	Póuh Kyùhn	包拳	包拳
Black Dragon Swing Tail	Hēilóngbǎiwěi	Hàk Lùhng Báai Méih	黑龙摆尾	黑龍擺尾
Inside Achievement	Nèigōng	Noih Gùng	内功	内功
Three Method Balancing Steam	Sānfǎhéngqì	Saàm Faat Hàhng Hei	三法衡气	三法衡氣
Pressing Heaven	Àntiān	On Tin	按天	按天
Pressing Earth	Àntǔ	On Tóu	按	按
Pressing Heaven, Earth	Àntiāntǔ	On Tin Tóu	按天	按天
Steam Sea	Qìhǎi	Hei Hói	气海	氣海
Man Center (Philtrum)	Rénzhōng	Yàhn Jung	人中	人中
Seal Hall	Yìntáng	Yan Tòhng	印堂	印堂
Relaxing, Calm Post	Sōngjìngzhuāng	Sang Jihng Jong	松静桩	鬆靜椿

Chapter 4: The Tools – Liniment and Bags

English	Pinyin (Mandarin)	Yale (Cantonese)	Simplified	Traditional
Falling, Beating Wine	Diēdǎjiǔ	Dit Da Jáu	跌打酒	跌打酒

Chapter 5: Iron Skills Training

English	Pinyin (Mandarin)	Yale (Cantonese)	Simplified	Traditional
Issue energy	Fajin	Faat Ging	发劲	發勁
Brave Tiger Scratching Sand	Měng-hǔzhuāshā	Máahng Fú Jáu Sà	猛虎抓沙	猛虎抓沙
Tiger Claw	Hǔzhuǎ	Fú Jaáu	虎爪	虎爪
Floating Palm	Fúzhǎng	Fauh Jeung	浮掌	浮掌

Chapter 6: Slap Strike for Iron Body

English	Pinyin (Mandarin)	Yale (Cantonese)	Simplified	Tradition
Patting, Hitting Achievement	Pāidǎgōng	Paak Dá Gùng	拍打功	拍打功

Chapter 8: Scatter Hands – Fighting Applications

English	Mandarin (Pinyin)	Cantonese (Yale)	Traditional	Simplified
Level Strike	Píngchuī	Ping Cheùih	平吹	平吹
Piercing Palm	Chāzhǎng	Chaap Jeúng	插掌	插掌
Seizing Hand	Lǔshǒu	Lóuh Sáu	擄手	擄手
Covering Palm	Gàizhǎng	Goi Jeúng	蓋掌	盖掌
Knee Press	Xīyā	Sàt Ngaat	膝壓	膝压
Hooking Leg	Gōutuǐ	Ngàu Téui	勾腿	勾腿
Sweeping Strike	Sǎochuī	Sou Cheùih	掃吹	扫吹
Detain Hand	Kòushǒu	Kau Sáu	扣手	扣手
Piercing Strike	Guànchuī	Gwun Cheùih	貫吹	贯吹

English	Mandarin (Pinyin)	Cantonese (Yale)	Traditional	Simplified
Wing Arm	Bǎngshǒu	Bóng Sáu	膀手	膀手
Embracing Waist, Crossing Back	Bàoyāoguòbèi	Póuh Yiù Gwo Bui	抱腰過背	抱腰过背
Horizontal Swing Leg	Héngbǎituǐ	Wáahng Báai Téui	橫擺腿	橫摆腿
Embracing Arm	Bàoshǒu	Póuh Sáu	抱手	抱手
Guard	Fáng	Fohng	防	防
Pressing Palm	Ànzhǎng	Jeúng	按	按掌
Throwing Elbow	Piězhǒu	Pit Jaáu	撇肘	撇肘
Planting Strike	Zāichuī	Jòi Cheùih	栽吹	栽吹
Positive Palm	Yángzhǎng	Yeùhng Jeúng	陽掌	阳掌

ABOUT THE AUTHOR

 Dr. Dale Dugas is a board-certified, state licensed Acupuncture Physician/Doctor of Oriental Medicine (AP/DOM) as well as a board-certified Chinese herbalist. His passion for traditional Asian medicinal practices arose in the late 1980s, while living in Iwate Prefecture, Northern Japan; working for the local Japanese Government in the Board of Education for Yamada township. There he was exposed to Japanese style Acupuncture and herbal medicine. He additionally holds a Masters in Acupuncture and Oriental Medicine, and a BA in Japanese Studies

Dr. Dugas has over 35 years of training in Chinese, Okinawan and Japanese martial arts, including Uechi-ryu Karate, Judo/Jujitsu, Jook Lum Tong Long Pai/Southern Mantis, Shuai Jiao, Xingyiquan, Baguazhang, Taijiquan and Internal/External Qigong systems. He began his martial arts journey as a young teenager and has traveled extensively to train privately and publicly in both Chinese martial arts and traditional Chinese medicinal systems. He is a highly trained proponent of traditional Dit Da Ke (Chinese trauma medicine) as well as Tieh Sha Zhang Gong (Iron Palm) and Tieh Be Shan Gong (Iron Vest). He teaches publicly and privately and treats patients in Tampa, Florida.

戰鬥鐵沙掌鐵功協衫協會

TAMBULI MEDIA

Excellence in Mind-Body Health & Martial Arts Publishing

Welcome to Tambuli Media, publisher of quality books on mind-body martial arts and wellness presented in their cultural context.

Our Vision is to see quality books once again playing an integral role in the lives of people who pursue a journey of personal development, through the documentation and transmission of traditional knowledge of mind-body cultures.

Our Mission is to partner with the highest caliber subject-matter experts to bring you the highest quality books on important topics of health and martial arts that are in-depth, well-written, clearly illustrated and comprehensive.

Tambuli is the name of a native instrument in the Philippines fashioned from the horn of a carabao. The tambuli was blown and its sound signaled to villagers that a meeting with village elders was to be in session, or to announce the news of the day. It is hoped that Tambuli Media publications will "bring people together and disseminate the knowledge" to many.

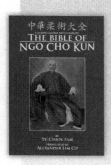 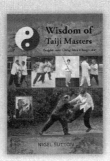 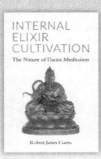 

TAMBULI MEDIA
Spring House, PA
TambuliMedia.com

戰鬥鐵沙掌鐵衫功協會

33701891R00097

Made in the USA
Middletown, DE
23 July 2016